The COACH'S JOURNEY

Volume I

True Stories of
Transformational
Experiences
with iPEC's Core
Energy Coaching™

Foreword by
BRUCE D SCHNEIDER
Founder, Institute for Professional Excellence in Coaching (iPEC)

The Coach's Journey, Volume I
Copyright ©2010 by Seed Word Communications LLC

Library of Congress Control Number: 2010916703
ISBN 978-0-9817603-3-9

Published by:
Seed Word Communications LLC
P.O. Box 16615
Tallahassee, FL 32317
Phone: +1.850.765.0386
www.seedword.com

Interior design and production: Alan Prescott
Cover design and illustration: Alan Prescott
prescott_alan@comcast.net
alanjayprescott@gmail.com
prescottdesignshop.com

Copyediting: Alan Prescott and Raechel Anderson

Introduction and Journey Guide: Michael Reddy, PH.D.
michael@reddyworks.com
www.reddyworks.com

Editorial team: Joseph Amanfu, Raechel Anderson,
Alan Prescott, Michael Reddy

Acknowledgments

In all fairness, I am dedicating this book to coach A-Mecca Goforth. Even though the story of her journey did not make it into this book, it was her bravery and unique way of connecting to our hearts, during that iPEC class in Tampa Bay, Florida, that birthed the inspiration for this book.

I have great respect for the spirit of abundance demonstrated by all contributing authors who have openly shared portions of their lives and work, some of which could easily be classified as intellectual property.

I appreciate the generous hours devoted by the editorial team comprised of: Raechel Anderson, Michael Reddy, and Alan Prescott. Alan designed the book's cover and internal layout, and performed copyediting duties as well.

I am grateful to Michael Port (www.michaelport.com) and Luke Iorio (www.ipeccoaching.com) for letting us print their opinions of this book on the back cover. I am humbled by the fact that Dr. Bruce D Schneider, Founder and Chairman of iPEC, put his stamp of approval on this project with the Foreword (*p. xi*). I was almost afraid to ask him to do it, but he demonstrated his usual spirit of giving, care, and love for iPEC graduates by saying, "Yes!" Thank you, Bruce.

My most special thanks go to Michael Reddy for his contributions above and beyond the call of duty. He generously gave of his time to:

> Research and write an informative **Introduction** (*p. xiii*) that sketches the evolution of modern professional coaching, iPEC's role in this, and points out both the amazing variety and some shared themes that appear in our stories;
>
> Read and appreciate our stories so as to produce summaries of their highlights and contexts—available now

as a kind of reader's "GPS" in the **Journey Guide** *(p. xxix)*;

Obtain Alan's services to design the cover and interior of the book (prescottdesignshop.com).

Michael Reddy's efforts significantly improved the value and readability of this collection.

I feel blessed to be associated with iPEC and everyone who was involved in this project.

Dr. Joseph Amanfu, PMP, CCP, MBCS, CTM, CPC, ELI-MP, Ph.D.
President & CEO, Seed Word Communications, LLC
www.seedword.com

TABLE OF CONTENTS

FOREWORD

Whether you skim the **Journey Guide** *(p. xxix)* to pick and choose your favorite stories, or read straight through it, I believe you will find the variety of people and situations depicted in this book both refreshing and, really, somewhat amazing. So many different kinds of lives and businesses play out within these pages, and even though they are all associated with our coach training here at iPEC, each person's transformation remains utterly unique.

There is a common theme to stories like these that I particularly enjoy and see, more often than you might think. The deep fulfillment people really seek in life can easily lie, not so much in plain sight, but rather around peculiar and unsuspected corners. Though individuals often take the first, sometimes hesitant steps on their voyages, with unclear orientation and heading, in hindsight, most everyone sees their own path as having unfolded perfectly.

Yet, not everyone moves forward when the path is not clear. What steers those who move on, anyway? What compass prompts going straight here or turning sharply over there? I am proud to say iPEC has refined its Core Energy Coaching™ Process over many years, to connect people with that precious internal guidance system. Eliciting deep values, felt purpose, innermost motivations, and real passions, our Core Energy Coaching connects these internal factors to an enriched array of alternative, external actions. It helps the client become self-aware, accountable, persistent, and balanced in carrying out the best of those actions.

From the synergy of this one-of-a-kind partnership, the "best" way forward—whatever odd turns it may involve—unfolds exactly as it should. For more and more people, this has become the gateway, not just to a different life, but to working and living happily "on fire." Playing the game of life with full, passionate engagement leads through the maze, to the right wonderful places. Ultimately, it becomes clear that, even as new challenges arise, the steady practice of playing that game full out is its own reward.

And then some people, as the transformation takes hold, take an additional step. They realize that their strongest joy and real destiny lie in furthering the transformation of others—in becoming coaches themselves. Here for you to enjoy and digest, at your leisure, are the largely unedited stories of a broad cross-section of these people. It is my hope that, as you see aspects of yourself in them, you will begin to embrace what is an increasingly accepted reality in today's world: coaching can very much help you set your own life happily "on fire" and could even be the career for which you've been looking.

Feel free to contact any of the co-authors or visit us at www.ipeccoaching.com. The thousands of professionals trained in Core Energy Coaching are changing the world, one person at a time.

Bruce D Schneider
Founder and Chairman of the Institute for Professional Excellence in Coaching (iPEC)

INTRODUCTION

Origins of *The Coach's Journey* and the History of Coaching

MICHAEL REDDY Ph.D., CPC, ELI-MP

INTRODUCTION

THIS BOOK AND ITS ORIGINS

The book you now hold in your hands is unusual. The contributors are largely not professional writers. Yet the pages that await you serve up drama, growth, tragedy, and triumph in abundance; and there are new and interesting perspectives to be enjoyed. No collecting anthologist put forth an intended topic, asking for and choosing among the contributions that resulted. Still, there is a central experience that unites all these stories. For, if the authors in this book selected themselves, they nevertheless did so because they all felt something deeply, genuinely transformative had happened to themselves and their lives.

They were completing their training to become coaches at the Institute for Professional Excellence in Coaching (iPEC). Immersed in the Institute's Core Energy Coaching™ process, both receiving it and learning to deliver it, the shifts they experienced were important enough to make them sit down, do the work, and try to describe the changes to the world.

The idea that there should be a book first came up in May 2009, at one of iPEC's Tampa Bay classes. A trainee, named A-Mecca Goforth, read out a poem. Her peer coach for the first twelve-week session had been Tim Durling, and the poem told of her experiences as this man worked with her to achieve her own most precious goals. Dr. Joseph Amanfu, another student, happened to own a publishing company. He stood up and suggested that the class should collaborate on a book; one that documented the amazing journeys on which so many of them found themselves. Later, in October, at iPEC's graduate training, the Energy

Leadership course, open also to other certified coaches, Joe extended the invitation to another receptive audience.

HOW TO READ IT—THE JOURNEY GUIDE

The life contexts, content, and writing styles of the stories in this book vary widely. For some, reading straight through (in alphabetical order by author) will be a refreshing treat. On the other hand, if you are like many these days, and are pressed for time, then you might want to consult the **Journey Guide** *(p. xxix)* to begin with. There you will find short, representative summaries of the background and highlights of each story.

It's likely that two, three, or four stories are going to speak more eloquently and precisely to your life than others. Whether it's innovative business situations, the resilience of super-moms, employment instability, or health crises, the **Guide** will lead you, first, to what interests you most. Alternatively, if you would like to view the panorama of all these journeys, spread out across just a few minutes, the **Guide** is good for that too.

WHO ARE THE AUTHORS?

In fact, that panorama is both broad and richly detailed. Of the twenty people who accepted Dr. Amanfu's invitation, thirteen are women and seven men. While the most common national and cultural roots are those of the mainland U.S., authors in this collection have either immigrated from, or spent substantial amounts of time in: Africa, Australia, Belgium, Germany, Korea, India, Iran, Israel and New Zealand.

Globalization and the geopolitical turbulence of our times are apparent in the stories. Samita Loomba *(p. 101)* came to the U.S. from an established, loving Indian family—and stayed. Now, most of that family lives here. Joe Amanfu *(p. 17)*, born to the Ewe tribe in Ghana, West Africa, says he still often thinks in his native language and translates into English. Judi Rhee Alloway *(p. 9)* is one of three hundred thousand orphans adopted by U.S. citizens in the course of the Korean War. Ronit Hakimi's *(p. 81)* family was forced out of Iran when the Shah fell, and once again out of Israel after the Palestinian Intifada uprisings.

Authors in this collection have held positions in such major companies as Hewlett-Packard, Bloomingdale's, Disney, NASA, and GlaxoSmithKline. The different industries and professions represented here range from healthcare, high tech, engineering, and education, to law, therapy, the performing arts, and financial management. Since this kind of background information was not requested, but only inserted when authors felt it relevant, the range here is probably even wider.

And, of course, the stories also speak of that most essential human occupation of all—the nurturing of families and children. Stephanie Davis *(p. 51)*, Ronit Hakimi *(p. 81)*, and Kari Lowrey *(p. 111)* all relate experiences of this kind. Most of our authors are healthy, but some were faced with serious challenges in this area. More on that in a moment.

WHAT DREW THESE AUTHORS TO COACHING?

That people from such different backgrounds and occupations should all find a kind of essential missing link in coaching is significant. Practiced well, the profession fills a broadly based human need, but what prompted the changes in our authors' lives? What qualities and support systems helped them to move, sometimes steadily, other times by fits and starts, successfully through the process? After all, difficulties and real fears do sometimes accompany substantial shifts. The different kinds of evolution apparent here fit roughly into three groups.

ORGANIC TRANSITIONS

To begin with, let's be clear. For some, the transition to coaching—to "being" a coach, in the case of iPEC training—is relatively smooth and natural. Tim Durling *(p. 61)* felt like he was born to be a life coach and just had to discover that this was now a profession, then acquire for himself a better array of techniques. Anthony Fasano *(p. 65)* was already helping to advance engineering careers. He just bonded very strongly with fellow coach trainees, realized he could help engineers a whole lot better, and yearned to do it full time.

Ed Abel *(p. 1)* and Tina Frizzell-Jenkins *(p. 73)*, both successful entrepreneurs, had specialized information and skills to deliver to clients and found (as many in the business world have) that coaching tools made a huge difference. Carol Juergensen Sheets *(p. 141)* was already a successful therapist. She moved into coaching when she decided to think a whole lot bigger about her career goals. The effort she expended to become media figure "Carol the Coach" was substantial and is very instructive. Read her story for sure if you, too, want to think big. But as portrayed, her transition does not sound like a crisis.

RISING FROM THE ASHES

At the other end of the spectrum, however, some authors' lives were upended completely. Their resilient, determined, positive response to what seemed, at first, to be impossible challenges turned disaster into rebirth. The most obvious causes of these upheavals were serious reversals in areas of career or health—or sometimes a combination of both.

Raechel Anderson *(p. 33)* was diagnosed with bipolar disorder, and Barbara Appelbaum *(p. 41)* felt half her body go numb in the first onset of multiple sclerosis. Not easy pills to swallow. Both of these brave women provide wonderful examples of how to deal creatively with serious health setbacks. If you cannot cure the condition, you can nevertheless, if you choose to, create a kind of new person—one whose shifted ideas of success and fulfillment are not blocked by the condition. Indeed, as we see in these stories, sometimes it is precisely experience with the condition that becomes the source of new fulfillment. Of course, Christopher Reeves's evolution from Superman to wheelchair-bound health crusader comes also to mind here.

Ronit Hakimi *(p. 81)* left her on-target career and initially fell into a deep depression after the birth of not one, but two special-needs children. Olivia, the youngest daughter of Stephanie Davis *(p. 51)*, developed a rare form of epilepsy. After various heart-wrenching recoveries and relapses, this ultimately led to having half of Olivia's brain removed. The Davis family's journey, described here, touches both the heights and the depths of human experience. And Michael Reddy (*p. 121*) left one position for another, only to see it disappear in the Crash, and then found himself nearly crippled by unexplained, untreatable foot pain.

SUPPORT IN THE CRUCIBLE

All of these authors found in iPEC's Core Energy Coaching™ process the understanding and behavioral tools to not only survive, but turn these setbacks into new lives full of acceptance, purpose and, yes, also new-found enjoyment. For this to be true of the company is not surprising—as we shall shortly see. Still, none of this is to say that other kinds of help, besides coaching, were not also in evidence in their lives.

Support from spouses and extended family appear to be crucial in several stories. Both good and bad examples of parents and grandparents make their contributions. Deep faith, spiritual traditions of various kinds, and strong positive outlooks instilled early in life—all these play significant roles in the strongly crisis-related transitions. Michael Reddy's journey (*p. 121*) even raises the question of whether significant support (or blocks) can arise from ancestral family members.

GATHERING IN THE THREADS

For other authors, the movement into coaching came about neither quite smoothly nor yet with any single, major crisis. For Sue Koch (*p. 87*), the pressures of extreme and unrewarding overwork in technology built across the years as her father, and then mother, passed away. Her movement was gradual. Kilian Kröll (*p. 93*) and Jaime Yordan-Frau (*p. 147*), both coincidentally involved in dance as a performing art, moved through a number of occupations with both successes and false starts. Finally, it seemed that coaching was the home base that could both sustain and bring their interests together. Consolidation is perhaps the best theme here.

Jennifer Barley (*p. 47*), also a veteran of high tech, walked instinctively along a curious path that led from desire for community, to a job as waitress, to extra pounds, to Weight Watchers as a trainer, and finally to coaching. Her story is a wonderful example of following one's intuitive heart to previously unsuspected sources of fulfillment. Kari Lowrey *(p. 111)* recreated herself twice—first as a health-oriented non-smoker, and then as a woman who could marry successfully and have a family. And finally, Judi Rhee Alloway *(p. 9)*, whose flamboyant, nomadic odyssey literally spans the globe, found peace, not only in coaching, but also in working with iPEC.

So What is Coaching Anyway?

In Appendix A *(p. 179)*, you will find a great deal of information on the topic of coaching, as formulated by the International Coaching Federation (ICF). It includes sections on what coaches do, why coaching is growing, how to choose a coach, how to be successful with one, and more. Consult this material as you find yourself drawn to it. It is concise, well presented, and will tune you in to one of the secrets of more and more highly successful people.

But for the moment, let's provide a brief overview. Interpersonal, behavioral coaching relies on the power of a unique, forward-looking, solution-focused partnership between coach and client. Different in specific ways from spouse, friend, mentor, consultant, therapist, and athletic coach *(see* "How is Coaching Distinct from Other Service Professions," *p. 180)*, the interpersonal coach is all about seeing the client move from merely functional in life to optimal, in the client's own terms.

Coaches consider clients the experts in their own lives, and themselves as masters of a thought-provoking and creative process—one that inspires and supports clients in maximizing their personal and professional potential. In fact, in the majority of cases, it is far easier to do this within the coaching partnership than without.

HOW DID COACHING EVOLVE?

Interpersonal coaching, as we know it today, grew from various streams of thought and practice influential in the later twentieth century. On the one hand, the psychological helping professions began to outgrow their exclusive emphasis on the medical model—with its "diagnosable" conditions that need to be "cured." Instead, seminal figures like Abraham Maslow and Carl Rogers argued that focusing on people's inborn potential for positive change also made profound sense.

Some, of course, do need "therapies" based on "what's wrong," but real behavioral challenges arise in the lives of a vastly greater number of people for whom this approach is not only unhelpful, but also demeaning and demoralizing. Raechel Anderson's success story *(p. 33)* is relevant again here. It suggests that, perhaps more often than we might think, even someone with a recognizable mental health diagnosis like "bipolar" does better with both approaches.

As momentum built, there were many contributions to this change. The ground-breaking hypnotic techniques of Milton Erickson, for instance, led to Neuro-linguistic Programming (NLP) and Solution-Focused Brief Therapy. Martin Seligman's later founding of positive psychology, as both an academic discipline and a means of self-help, is another major landmark. Meanwhile, organizational consultants, management trainers, and industrial psychologists were busy figuring out how to get better work out of already functional people—and, if possible, keep them well and happy at the same time.

And with roots as far back as Napoleon Hill (*Think and Grow Rich*) and Norman Vincent Peale (*The Power of Positive Thinking*), self-help books and "transformational" trainings brought into popular consciousness the potential uses of "mental reprogramming" and other self-actualizing behaviors. Among the trainings, those of Werner Erhard, José Silva, and Anthony Robbins, to mention a few, contributed much to this evolving awareness.

Thomas Leonard and the ICF

All these streams coalesced, most prominently in 1992, when Thomas Leonard (a former financial planner who loved RVs) more or less created the profession of life coaching when he founded Coach University. Also a pioneer in the area of teleconferencing, he showed an expanding circle of practitioners that both group classes and private sessions could be delivered by phone directly, from home to home. This meant that coaches could live and work pretty much anywhere.

In 1995, Leonard went on to found the International Coaching Federation. This professional association now has over thirteen thousand members, offers credentials to qualified coaches, and conducts research on the effectiveness of coaching. In 1998, a graduate of Coach University, Dr. Patrick Williams, founded the first coaching school dedicated to teaching the tools of coaching to mental-health professionals. And in 1999, Bruce D Schneider founded iPEC.

Coaching Today—From Traditional to Transformational

Modern professional coaching, says Luke Iorio, CEO of iPEC, is delivered across a spectrum that ranges from traditional to transformational. Traditional coaching begins by bringing the power of positive partnership mostly to the client's or business's "outer" needs and wants. The coach helps the client set goals, prioritize, plan, and be accountable to someone for carrying plans out. Towards the middle of the spectrum, there may also be more highly skilled acknowledgment and validation of client feelings, and better tools for changing behaviors.

But there remain deeper questions of what constitutes real fulfillment, the meaning of one's life or business mission in the world today—in other words, the "why" of these outer goals. In traditional coaching, these might not get looked at that closely. And when blocks arise, those underlying personal or structural impediments to growth and progress, often not much more than some superficial cheerleading, gets applied to them.

TRANSFORMATIONAL COACHING GOES DEEPER

Transformational coaching, on the other hand, along with the outer, always keeps one eye on the "inner." In today's world, a lot of active people suffer from what Iorio, in his business classes, calls "three-hundred-sixty-degree overwhelm." So much is going on. There are just too many obligations, expectations, and interests to keep up with. Inner feelings of fulfillment get very easily lost. And this is problematic, since the best cure for the miasma of Information Age overwhelm is a deeply felt, clearly understood alignment with one's core passions.

Tapping into these passions creates a kind of steady, internal energy that makes aligned activities, even if they involve long hours, seem effortless. Seligman's positive psychology follows Mihaly Csikszentmihályi (who coined the term) in calling this the experience of "flow." Beyond the energy boost, core level alignment lets one know what to let go of—which priorities can be lowered or dropped entirely.

In transformational coaching, moreover, the commitment to maintaining a positive outlook is both deeper and more grounded. A great many people would have far more of their dreams if there were not blocks, inner habits of thought and feeling, that stand squarely in the way. Superficial, "just do it" cheerleading does not really acknowledge and deal with these. Behaviors don't change in ways that are substantial or sustainable.

Short of diagnosable mental conditions, transformational coaches watch for and isolate different kinds of blocks, and have tools to help clients get past them. Deeper blocks are often the remains of defenses against past suffering. Others are negative generalizations about "the way things are," and these can be turned around. They started out as defenders, as allies, and can be reframed to become allies once again in the current situation. Or they were true enough at one point, but not any longer.

DEEPER THAN DENIAL

All the same, it is important to acknowledge that the whole edifice of positive thinking is often attacked, sometimes with justification, for being too "Polyannaish"—just simply too blindly optimistic. This brings up the problem of denial. When you suppress awareness of the facts of reality, of course it's easy to be optimistic, but it usually only makes those problematic facts grow larger and more dangerous. Think of the active alcoholic who claims, "Who, me? I don't have a problem."

Far from engaging in mere cheerleading, transformational coaching approaches this problem head on. And the way it does this embodies perhaps one of the deeper meanings of "transformational" here. The coach works to bring the client around to the perspective that setbacks and adverse conditions—fully acknowledged, looked at square in the face—always signal new opportunities. And that a rich and success-filled life—part of the path to what Seligman calls "authentic happiness"—comes about when one refocuses steadily and accurately on those opportunities. They are there to find when you become committed to looking for them.

In place of denial, which is passive and closes off, this kind of coaching seeks to instill an open, intelligent habit of dynamic reframing. Plans and actions shift accordingly and never cease to marry goals to actual reality. With really large setbacks, the feelings of grief or loss need more time to be honored, so the reorientation is slower, but the end result is the same. Positivity this deep takes some learning, some clearing of old habits, and very often the support of a coach—but the results are always life altering.

BRUCE D SCHNEIDER—FROM TRAGEDY TO iPEC

It should come as no surprise that even people in real crises could come to iPEC's training and find so much of what they need. In a real sense, Bruce Schneider's founding of iPEC can be traced back to a massive, life-threatening crisis in his own life. With his body damaged so extensively that doctors considered it hopeless, he lay nearly comatose in a hospital bed and had a transcendent, near-death experience.

Something within him belied the condition of his bones and

organs. That something was well and strong, still very much connected to life, and would recover. He just knew it. Indeed, not only would it recover—it would turn this "terrible" accident into the opportunity that shaped a life of wide-ranging and profound exploration. If he could do this, then, really, what kinds of surprising things were human beings capable of? And how could they come to better access these abilities?

It is interesting to compare Schneider's biography to the genesis of coaching. In fact, his background pretty much spans the gamut of the ideas and disciplines that birthed this profession. He studied business at William Paterson College, and psychotherapy and social work at Rutgers. His credentials include hypnotherapy and Reiki. As evidenced by his first book, *Relax—You're Already Perfect*, he looked rather deeply into the nature of human reality, while achieving a doctorate in metaphysics from the American Institute for Holistic Theology.

Schneider was a senior instructor in the transformational Silva Mind Control trainings, and used his evolving knowledge of how to achieve peak performance to set home run records in semi-professional softball. From athletics to human potential, from the psychological helping professions to success in business—so many of the root disciplines of interpersonal coaching are found in Schneider's vita.

iPEC's Foundation Principles

The distillations of all this passionate searching are apparent in the sweep and depth of the training materials Schneider and his team have created. In addition to all the relevant skills and processes, iPEC's Core Energy Coaching™ is based on a set of "Foundation Principles." These are, as the manual puts it, "a life philosophy, and a way of being...a way to walk the talk."

While it is possible to quibble with a few of these, or wish them stated differently, or argue that some of them overlap— these thirty-three concise, carefully explained and illustrated epigrams capture the cutting edge of an evolving understanding of human consciousness. They are not theoretical abstractions penned by some over-intellectual academic. Instead, they encapsulate deceptively simple nuggets of deep truth, resonant perspectives that anyone can take with him or her into the trenches of life—and learn from over and over again. And they reflect "ways of engaging with life" typical of people with high levels of awareness and fulfillment.

THE ENERGY LEADERSHIP ASSESSMENT

In fact, the Foundation Principles are practical and real enough that iPEC can actually produce measurements from them. The company has evolved something like the Myers-Briggs or DISC personality evaluations, except that the Energy Leadership Assessment reveals how a person's energies and consciousness are typically distributed among seven types or levels. So, unlike these other assessments, which are static, this one is dynamic. It shows the changes as a person grows.

iPEC's follow-up surveys have established a very real correlation between changes in these levels and how much satisfaction and enjoyment a person is getting out of life. What this comes down to is unique. The higher your energy levels are, the better things go for you. There is real evidence that, the more you can internalize the Foundation Principles, the happier and more successful (in your own terms) you are likely to be. Schneider's best-selling book, *Energy Leadership: Transforming Your Workplace and Your Life from the Core*, introduces the seven energy levels via the story of a small business owner who is coached towards understanding and practicing them.

THE iPEC TRAINING PROGRAM

Quite obviously, in terms of the spectrum ranging from traditional to transformational coaching methods, iPEC is really working to pioneer the transformational end. Over three hundred fifty hours of trainings, teleclasses, peer study groups, peer coaching, mentor coaching, and both written and oral exams are all aligned towards the same end. Trainees need to undergo the transformation first, in order to induce it later in their clients. Just how successful the program can be, you may judge for yourself as you take in the spontaneous evaluations expressed by authors in this collection.

Beyond this, iPEC excels in imparting marketing, sales, and entrepreneurial business skills to fledgling coaches who are not already employed in corporate settings. A business Quick Start program is available at no cost to any who choose to take it. Ed Abel *(p. 1)*, with his vast experience teaching business owners, takes the lead in this area. The capstone of the program is then the graduate Energy Leadership training. iPEC students, along with other certified coaches, learn to explain, market, and administer this innovative assessment to clients—and especially how to review the results with them. Some of the kinds of coaching businesses set up by authors in this collection are contained in Business Profiles *(pp. 155–177)*. It is a fascinating array.

LEARN AND ENJOY

You will hear much about the magic of transformational coaching in the months and years to come. We are all enmeshed in the fast-paced complexities of a rapidly evolving Information Age. More and more of us are less employees and more quasi-independent knowledge workers, micro-entrepreneurs with a shifting array of skill sets. High-quality interpersonal coaching will become the "no brainer" of the decade. As we come to understand the pathways from bored and merely existing to passionate and high-functioning better and better, this uniquely supportive partnership turns out to be a key element.

Whether your interest is in finding the right coach, or becoming a great one yourself, the journeys related in this collection will both move and inform you. Aligning inner values and passions with well-planned and executed outer actions creates extraordinary, sustainable success. Read on and enjoy. Watch that happen again and again as you move through *The Coach's Journey*.

MICHAEL REDDY, Ph.D., CPC, ELI-MP

JOURNEY GUIDE

GUIDE

What's in
the Stories?

MICHAEL REDDY PH.D., CPC, ELI-MP

JOURNEY GUIDE
What's in the Stories?

Here's a man who built a $36-million-a-year healthcare business. Finding it unmanageable, he sold it off and built another, very different one. And then another. And still more. Ultimately, he found himself on a quest to discover what makes smaller, entrepreneurial businesses grow and prosper—yet also remain a sane and sustainable experience for their owners and executives. Understanding and packaging that knowledge, Ed thought, would surely help a lot of struggling owners. Okay, so he does that, only to find that sharing all that precious knowledge is not so easy. Entrepreneurs are busy, distracted, and don't "get it." Something's still missing from the process. Learning how to coach, it turns out, especially with the tools iPEC offers, provides the missing link. The delivery system is now complete, helping hundreds of "SkillPreneur®" and iPEC graduates to thrive. Meet Ed Abel—"the better business builder."

There's an acronym "OAKs," which means "overseas adopted Koreans." There are three hundred thousand such adopted orphans spread "like dandelion seeds" across the continents. Judi Alloway arrived in the U.S. shortly after her birth, and has been on the move ever since. In this story, she traces a saga of studies, travels, accomplishments, and crisis-rich adventures that stretches first literally around the world—and then back and forth across the Pacific several times. Gifted in many ways, she is someone in-terested in peaceful international relations, leadership, social justice, and the legacies of her Korean origins. Like other high-achieving people with broad backgrounds, she has found a home base in coaching.

Imagine yourself a senior international program manager for Hewlett-Packard. You have recently been honored as a top performer. Originally from West Africa, you have become not only a citizen of the world, but also a leader respected in the corporate circles of eleven different countries. Still, the day comes when you return from a highly successful, three-year assignment in South Africa to find yourself—along with other outstanding people and an entire product line—suddenly no longer a priority for the company. The very next Sunday, a guest minister in your church stops in the middle of his sermon, points unexpectedly at you, and blurts out, "Get ready, God is calling you." There are lucrative offers overseas with Hewlett-Packard, but leaving the U.S. just doesn't feel right. What exactly do you do? Is becoming a full-time coach a reasonable option?

After a couple of particularly tough years, Raechel Anderson was diagnosed with bipolar disorder. Useful life—like law school and her job—seemed over. Still, the treatments began to kick in, and she began trying some things. They didn't all work out, but there were visible learning and progress in each one. Accepting some limitations, overcoming others, she eventually built a successful consulting business, and became a national speaker on the subject of mental illness. Still, something was missing from the picture. That's when she started talking to a life coach.

5 Facing Adversity: Discovering a Gift

There came a weekend when her food tasted like tin. Barbara Appelbaum realized with shock that the entire right side of her body was numb and she had lost partial vision in her left eye. Three weeks of tests and consultations finally resolved into the unthinkable—she had multiple sclerosis, a chronic, potentially debilitating disease. For a year she went about her life as normally as possible, not letting this affect her steady performance as Senior Director of Development for a foundation. And guess what? They laid her off. For so many, this would be a devastating blow that would crush the spirit and leave mostly a broken person who would retreat inwards. But lessons taught by her father, practicing healing prayer, and the desire to move on and help other people stricken with adversity made all the difference in Barbara's life.

6 From High Tech to Life Tech

Pathways to the life of our dreams sometimes start off in curious directions. Jennifer Barley walked away from twelve years of grueling high-tech employment and got support from her husband for "finding her passion"—but had little idea what it was. The first inner message seemed to be "get closer to your community." So she became the morning cook at a local diner and met—everybody. Great—but still no clarity. Oh, but actually quite a few more pounds did find their way onto her body. Hmm... That led to Weight Watchers and to eventually becoming a Weight Watchers group leader. Meanwhile, she's off studying interior design, because, well, maybe that's her passion. But before long, something magical seems to be happening at the Weight Watchers meetings she leads. She's changing people's lives. Hold on a minute—that's really fun!

7 Team Olivia

Here's a family traveling in Guatemala on the occasion of adopting a third child, born in that country. Suddenly their youngest natural child, Olivia, is shaking uncontrollably while taking a shower. And it's not stopping. Her mother, Stephanie Davis, holds her in the shower stall for what seems like forever. So begins a heart-wrenching story that leads ultimately through the long, dark tunnel of recovery and relapse, to an unthinkable place—half of Olivia's brain will have to be removed. And yet, for all the tears and struggle, this story is also astonishingly positive. You watch a family, under the guidance of Stephanie Davis, form up into something that genuinely deserves the name "Team Olivia." Everyone contributes something, and Olivia reaches always for life and wellness. If there is a question that stands out at the end of this testimony to love, faith, and human determination, it is perhaps this—who is the greater heroine here, Stephanie, the mother, or Olivia, her daughter? The family is producing a book about this experience and reaches out now to help others who are afflicted.

8 There's a Coach in My Mirror!

One Friday evening, Tim Durling went to a conference in Tampa featuring speakers like Wayne Dyer and Marianne Williamson. Dyer's keynote left him profoundly excited. On Saturday, he found he just couldn't leave to attend his normal church service. Various upbeat strangers he spoke with kept asking him if he was a life coach. One woman, who was a life coach, told him he was a natural. Still, Tim had always been a corporate IT guy, focused on software, help desks, and business solutions. On Sunday, it all came to a head in front of the booth of a vendor who sold T-shirts. On the shirts, short affirmations were printed backwards—so that the wearer, looking in a mirror, could read them. After much deliberation, Tim chose his shirt and, with it, his new life. Seeing himself in a mirror, it read, "I change lives."

9 Better Bonding, Better Careers

Anthony Fasano is a man who went through a very uncomfortable hazing process to join a college fraternity. Some guys quit. But what he remembers most about the experience is the bonding that took place among those who didn't quit. Then he had the courage to leave all his "new brothers" and take off for a wonderfully broadening six months in Europe. As an engineer, he fast-tracked his own and many others' careers. But still, that bonding experience lingers in his mind, and somehow, he's still searching for his place. iPEC training, it turns out, forms bonds with fellow coaches "one hundred times stronger," and now, he fast-tracks careers on a full-time basis.

10 Grace and Life Purpose

Was this author learning-challenged as a child? Well, maybe so, but grace and extra-hard work made her a class representative early on. They also got her through a tough engineering degree and into a great job with NASA. Is a banker discriminating on the loan she deserves? Grace and a congressman turned that around. NASA doesn't think she's got what it takes to be a coach? Grace and the iPEC training she took on her own convinced them they were wrong. Couple grace with life purpose, says Tina Frizzell-Jenkins, and awesome things will occur! She has designed and built a home, started a couple of businesses, and raises two children. She particularly favors the "three step" coaching process for keeping herself and others moving towards those cherished goals.

11 Who Will Fix the Fixer?

Ronit Hakimi, born in Tehran, was four years old when the Shah of Iran was deposed. Mom packed two suitcases for herself and four children and fled to start life over as a refugee in Israel. Dad stayed behind two years, but still had to leave most of their assets behind. Young Ronit, precocious and intensely aware of her parents' suffering, took on a new way of being. If she can just be perfect, and just start to fix everything—maybe they will be happier. Ronit was fifteen when the Palestinian Intifada uprising forced another emigration—this time to the U.S. The family endured another major culture shock. Still, Ronit graduated from college and became an executive at Bloomingdale's. She was at the top of her game and fixing everything really well.

However, marriage brought, not one, but two special-needs children. Oh, my God. She quits her job, but still her girls cannot be "fixed." She can only love and try to care for them. A deep depression sets in, which echoes her own and her family's loss of two cultural homes and lives. Out of the depths of this depression, this resilient and determined woman slowly realizes something profound—that the one person she has never fixed is herself. As that actually begins to happen, along comes coaching. How perfect! In coaching, you can help quite a bit, but the name of the game is: everyone really does fix him/herself.

12 Let the Madness Cease
SUE KOCH

Meet Sue Koch, Miss Tech-Success—she had the job, the salary, the car, and the condo. Oh, and yes, also the fourteen-hour days, the stress, and considerable, pure misery. Then, one day—Dad died, before she could get to his side. Afterwards, plunging back into even more work, Sue found avoidance failing her. Deeply depressed, sitting alone on the couch one day, she thought, "I can't go on this way! I don't care anymore." What was it that shoved her up, into running clothes, and off to the gym that day? Later on, she will swear it was her dead father. She found iPEC, began coach training, and realized, "What I care about is people!"

Still, Mom needed financial support. And what about that lifestyle? So, the Senior V.P. of Operations stayed on the job, and added caring for an ailing mother to the marathon workdays. But there was no coaching in what seemed like a truly toxic work environment. Then, a last, "easy" operation to save Mom ended up killing her. In the aftermath, back in coach training, comparing her mother's life to her own, something shocking creeps into Sue's awareness. "It's not merely the loss of my parents lives I am grieving now," she thinks. "It's the loss of my own… And for the first time, at thirty-eight years old, I am about to discover who I am."

13 Coaching Academic Creatives
Kilian Kröll arrived in the U.S. from Austria and Germany in 1997 to study at Haverford College. An English major, active in modern dance, and member of the LGBT community—he parleyed his multicultural perspectives into a rich and nourishing four years. Yet, graduating with honors, he came to realize he had gotten his "A's" the stupid way. He had traded off creativity and risk for the sure good grade. He explored for a while, then settled into a teacher training program for the public schools. Once in the classroom, however, he experienced that same sticking point. The price of the sure-thing job was a stultifying, institutional atmosphere where not much genuine teaching took place.

More exploring followed, including a stint helping to produce a large-scale dance project. As part of this, at an international "Cultural Studies" conference in London, Kilian saw the end result of the pressures against originality and risk placed on creative academics. Too many of the most successful and famous academics involved in the arts felt stifled and out of touch with their own unique gifts. A natural gadfly and coach, Kilian challenges and entices, inspiring a return to those gifts, wherever possible. After the conference, when he enrolls in coach training at iPEC, his specialty is obvious to him. He helps right-brained creatives thrive in left-brained institutions.

14 A Legacy of Love
Samita Loomba, a young woman from a well-positioned, very loving Indian family, arrives in the States, at first, to attend graduate school. The university works differently, decent vegetarian food is hard to find, and shopping malls are beyond imagining. She stays here afterwards, goes to work for a telecom company,

and begins to lead a bicultural life. On the Indian side, a properly arranged, parent-selected marriage simply does not work. And dating is not a skill she grew up with. As an American, she tries to help a relative, falsely accused in a financial scandal, who is nevertheless eventually declared guilty and deported. How is it that these bad things happen to good people? Her vision of herself as a caretaker is threatened. How do you think Samita will respond?

15 From Single and Smoker to Coach and Mom

Kari Lowrey was a smoker most of her life. To many, her life as a published poet and very successful leadership trainer seemed enchanted. She, on the other hand, had always wanted children. Except she only seemed able to date men with tortured souls. Watching her grandmother (also a smoker) die slowly in intensive care was the last straw. She changed her lifestyle completely. As part of this change, in touch with some coaching techniques already in her profession, Kari found iPEC and chose to become a professional coach. The program for her was transformational in a number of ways. Early on, she was asked to become an iPEC trainer. Beyond that, she shares the story of how she became the right woman to find her right man and have that child she had always wanted.

16 Who Defines Your Success?

Julie McManus thinks of herself as a corporate dropout. An early position in management, graduate school, training others in Australia and New Zealand, and a couple of vice presidencies—all failed to keep her interest. Unhappy and searching, she began working with a coach. Contrary to her expectations, this person had no answers for her—rather only the right questions. For whom have you been doing all these things? What would you like to do for yourself? Who are you anyway? What followed was six months of amazing and very different activities. Julie is still not totally clear about what success means, but she's sold on the process for figuring it out. It's coaching, and she's looking forward to helping others with it as well.

17 Feet First

Meet Michael Reddy, Ph.D., as he packs up his office. He's leaving a ten-year stint in upper management with a small company. And, looking back on a career spanning decades—with periods in business, academics, and a long commitment to teaching Native American spirituality—he has some very mixed feelings. While Michael has always been overtly successful, the endeavors he cared most about mostly seemed to stumble right at the edge of his personal goals. Months pass and, unexpectedly, mysterious pain in his feet threatens to cripple him. After nine months of different efforts to find healing or even a diagnosis all fail, at the edge of despair, he discovers something new—systemic, family constellation work. From this perspective, it seems the foot pain, and earlier reversals as well, are the expression of a deep but misplaced connection to the sufferings of his war veteran father.

Amazed and fascinated, Michael finds that "giving his father's pain back to him" dramatically improves his feet. He becomes determined to learn to facilitate constellation work. But the long months of pain and stress have left their mark. Unable to work for nearly a year, physically and emotionally debilitated, his old personality lies in ashes around him. He knows he needs some way to seriously retrain and rebuild. With long experience of various therapies and personal-growth techniques, he turns to iPEC coach training to provide this. The results are little short of magic. He emerges with, not one, but two complementary, cutting-edge tools for energizing success in people's lives.

18 There's Gotta Be a Way

Growing up in the closely knit, ethnic part of a Midwestern steel-producing town, Deborah Sakelaris enjoyed family celebrations, teamwork in high-school sports, and solid spiritual roots. College included time in Europe and a job as resident assistant. After discovering an aptitude for training at Disney in Florida, she became director of wellness for a nonprofit, and later traveled the country as a trainer of new franchise owners. Her first exposure to coaching was through the Coaches Training Institute. This gave her the basic tools to strike out in various new directions and start her own coaching business. Two years in, however, she discovered iPEC and realized there were far better tools she could master. Her motto for life goes back to challenges faced with her high-school best friend. As they would always say—"there's gotta be a way!"

19 Carol the Coach

At the beginning of the new millennium, after thirty years as a therapist, Carol Juergensen Sheets chose three new goals: to write a book, write a weekly newspaper column, and host a personal-growth radio show. With a huge supply of persistence and, now and then, a dash of "fake it till you make it"—she achieved all of these during the first five years of the decade. The story she tells about how she did this is seriously instructive for anyone with large, passionate ambitions. She came to iPEC to deepen her coaching skills, attracted by its solid psychological underpinnings. Currently, she's setting her sights on *Oprah* and Sirius Radio. Some of her columns have been combined into two manuals of personal-growth exercises. Meet and be inspired by "Carol the Coach."

20 Life as a River of Passion
Jaime Yordan-Frau describes himself as a "gypsy dreamer" until around age thirty. After graduate work in psychology, he walked out of his first job to participate in a forty-day retreat in the mountains of New Mexico. Emerging with a surprising passion for dance, he pursued this and arts administration for six years. Then something changed for him again. Shifting to corporate sales, he rose swiftly through the ranks to become chief of staff for a company president. But twelve years in, stagnation and then company politics have Jaime chafing once again. How long can

the river of passion within this dedicated and accomplished follower of dreams be dammed up? Not very long. Two weeks after his research convinces him coaching is the new watershed—he gets an undeserved pink slip. At iPEC training, it's clear the river is pouring happily into its new channel. Among his coaching business goals now, Jaime wants to shift our educational system. Let's prepare our young, he argues, to do well in life, as opposed to just later on in more school.

MICHAEL REDDY, Ph.D., CPC, ELI-MP

The Better Business Builder

ED ABEL

About Ed Abel

For more than three decades, I have been learning how to build a successful, thriving business. At age twenty-four, with a $5,000 loan and the energy and passion of a young entrepreneur, I was ready to take on the world. And I did, only to emerge seven years later at the top of a $36-million organization with 585 employees. Inspired by the challenges that led me to this success, I went on to build other multimillion-dollar businesses, yet I missed the passion that I experienced "in the trenches" of my formative years.

Determined to find a way to educate and advise others in the construction and sustainability of a vital business, I founded ABEL Business Institute. Over the course of this process, I developed The SkillPreneur® Business System, a systematic approach to the construction, maintenance and growth of a business—an approach that has become the philosophy and methodology of ABEL Business Institute.

This journey led me to become an adjunct professor of entrepreneurial studies at New York University (NYU), as well as the director of the business division at the world-class Institute for Professional Excellence in Coaching (iPEC). At iPEC, I am responsible for supporting the graduate coaches in their business-development process.

Before I was a coach

Before I became a business coach, I was a skilled IV nurse. What I loved about that career was my ability to truly help people and

1

to lift their spirits during a difficult time. It was tremendously fulfilling. While I loved my work, there was always a part of me that wanted to do more and be more—not to be chained to an inflexible schedule or a flawed operation.

Being inside that industry as a service provider, I clearly knew what the companies were doing wrong. They did not place enough emphasis on the skill level of the service providers they employed so that they could ensure that their clients were receiving the best possible care. When I left my job, it was because I knew I could do it better.

Because I excelled at my work, I decided that I would take my skills, along with my passion for helping people, and start my own business. I believed that I could create a better company than the organization I worked for, so when opportunity knocked—to the tune of a $5,000 loan from my parents—I grabbed it.

The start of something big

As I started building my company, I did an excellent job promoting the service component. So great, in fact, that from morning to night, I worked as a skilled IV nurse, running around to all of my patients' houses, providing my service. However, I was responsible for more than just providing the service. I had to keep the company running, too, i.e. paying bills, advertising, ordering supplies, etc. On the weekends, I would spend my time catching up. I would take care of billing, developing processes, scheduling, and calling clients.

As the business grew to a certain point, I no longer had time to market. I felt like I was a mouse on a spinning wheel, running as fast as I could go, but not getting anywhere. The good news is that my business took off and turned an immediate profit. If you equate profit with success, then I was tremendously successful. The truth is that, after a brief encounter with euphoria, I came crashing down to earth. I was miserable.

I was desperately missing work/life balance. I was simply moving from one day to the next, trying to keep everything under a respectable amount of control. In order to grow my business, I poured money into it. Unfortunately, money was flying out as fast as it was coming in, so I worked, sometimes eighteen to twenty hours a day. I was committed, no matter what, to making it work.

Instead of leading my business into the future, I was stuck dealing with the day-to-day tasks of running the business to the point where the business owned me, not the other way around. I had the marketable skill I needed to sell my service, but I had learned the hard way that it takes more than skill to run a business. I discovered that I was lacking the knowledge necessary to create an independent and profitable enterprise. I knew nothing about bookkeeping or cash flow, other than praying that enough money would come in to cover the urgent bills for the week.

I knew how to be a great IV nurse; I did not know how to build a great company. I did not have the knowledge and experience I needed to take care of all the other factors of running the business. To add to my stress, I found myself making decisions in areas where I had little or no experience, like human resources, payroll, or sales and marketing. Like fires, problems I never anticipated flared up everywhere.

I was completely lost when it came to knowing how to market; how to follow up with new prospects; how to communicate with referral sources; how to create and build relationships; how to manage payroll; how to hire and fire employees; how to train employees and how to develop policies and procedures. In fact, when I first started my business, I didn't even know I needed a special business license to offer my services until I got a knock on my door from an official asking to see it. I had to pay a fine and, of course, obtain a license.

My education on how to run my business was through trial and error—often more error than anything else. There was no book or step-by-step process for me to follow, and there was no one out there teaching others how to build successful, viable businesses.

Seven years later, my business had grown to 585 employees. My managers would look to me for advice and solutions to problems. My response to them was based on gut instinct, not sound business practices. I did not have any formal training or education that prepared me to run this organization.

My company grew because it provided a great service; however, it had no direction, no business plan, and no real goals— other than to grow the business. Neither it nor I had a strategic outlook, and the executive team spent no time forecasting and planning. We just dealt with the urgent fires that continually appeared and prayed that we would get through another day. It was certainly a non-strategic approach to building a business.

After seven years of sleepless nights, constantly worrying about what the next crisis would be, and getting up earlier and earlier every morning to try to get some work done before the new day's demands started, I knew it was time to sell the business. My dream had turned into a nightmare. I reached the point where I was simply trying to stay afloat and keep my head above water, but in truth, I was drowning.

From the outside, the company looked great. We looked like a big business with a great business model. No one knew what I was going through trying to keep everything together. Even though my business was earning revenues of $36 million with nearly six hundred employees, it was failing. I had not surrounded myself with enough knowledgeable people and I was unable to keep up with the changes in the industry.

You see, I was too busy being in my business. I could not see the long-term needs of my company, because I was too busy dealing with the daily demands of the business. The worst part of the situation was that I knew I needed help but I did not know where to turn. This was long before the days of the Internet, where I could just search for people to help me with my business. I was alone.

What led me to coaching?
It was not until after I sold the business in 1992 that I uncovered the painful truth: When I launched my business, I was not the entrepreneur I believed I was. I possessed the passion, purpose and perseverance that were needed to build my business, but I didn't have the business acumen to translate that power back into long-term, independent financial success.

But I had learned a great deal along the way, and I knew there were thousands of other business owners who were suffering a similar experience, alone and unsure of what direction to take and how to get there. These business owners could benefit from my guidance. The insights I had gained in building my business could help others avoid the same costly and painful mistakes.

I had developed a new passion: to be a resource to other business owners who were going it alone and did not know where to turn to find the guidance they needed to build their businesses successfully. I wanted to be a resource for them, although I still felt that I needed to prove—to myself—that I had what it took to build a successful, viable, independent business.

Through my experience, I had developed a working theory that there were specific principles and practices that could be employed to better guarantee the success of any business in any industry. I wanted to prove to myself that my theory had value. Since the best way to prove a theory is to test it in different situations, I spent many years creating, building, buying, selling, and closing different businesses in a variety of industries. It was important to expand my experience beyond skilled nursing and prove to myself that the principles and practices I had developed could be implemented in any business, in any industry.

Over the course of two decades, I developed more than a dozen successful businesses, two of them multimillion-dollar enterprises. Over time, I learned what it takes to develop and grow businesses in a variety of industries and overcome whatever obstacles stood in my way. I did everything from preparing a business to go public to building businesses with the ability to be duplicated through franchising.

These experiences provided first-hand knowledge of what made businesses work and what made them fail. I discovered that businesses failed, primarily, because the owner is too emotionally attached to the business to be able to see what needs to be done for the good of the business. Business after business, I honed my techniques and created a clearly defined path to success through the use of a methodical, step-by-step approach that is adaptable to any industry and that ensures the capability of success.

In essence, I had proven my theory. This unique set of principles and practices could be applied in nearly any business situation, in nearly any industry, to create viable, independent, profitable enterprises. Yet, even as I found success and satisfaction through these endeavors, I still felt that something was missing. I was searching for my purpose in the world. Was my purpose just to build businesses? How could I give back? How could I use my education and experience to help others?

Around that time, I met a woman who worked as a life coach. I had had no idea the profession of coaching existed. I connected with her so strongly and was so excited about how she contributed to others, that I immediately started researching the industry. Becoming a certified coach was exactly what I was seeking. It would qualify me to follow my passion: to teach, educate and guide other business owners in building sustainable, independent, profitable businesses.

> *"How could I give back? How could I use my education and experience to help others?"*

I had a high level of knowledge that I could share with other business owners. Every business needs leadership skills, marketing panache, operations experience, sales techniques and the ability to build relationships. On top of that, they needed an understanding of cash flow and money management. I knew that if I could teach business owners these critical skills, they could build more efficient businesses and enjoy a better life.

When I launched my coaching business, my initial challenge was illustrating to business owners why they needed my services. I would meet a new client, and they would be impressed with what I was able to accomplish in my business development, but their question would always be, "What can you do for me?"

The clients were not identifying with the level of pain I had in my business—the level of pain I knew they had as well. Nor could they relate to the joy that could come from working with someone who had been there before, who could guide them on their journey.

In order to help business owners identify with my services and to help them understand themselves better, I developed the identity of a SkillPreneur. SkillPreneurs are individuals with talent and expert ability in a specific art, trade, field, or technique that is acquired or developed through training and experience; but these individuals are unfamiliar with the methodology necessary to create an independent, sustainable, and profitable business.

I then created the SkillPreneur Business System, a systematic approach that will educate and guide a new business owner through the process of creating, maintaining, and growing a business. This unique system has been designed to educate the individual on the business skills required for success, provide step-by-step actions to follow, and provide accountability throughout the process to further ensure success.

My approach when coaching

Technically, I am a business coach, but I often think of myself more as a business advisor and mentor. My approach with business owners is to help them discover what they ultimately want from the business. This starts to establish, for business owners, an understanding of what the business means to them, and then slowly moves them away from *being* their business. I guide them to think of the business as a separate entity, which allows them to step back from their day-to-day actions and gain a wider view of the business, their industry and the direction they want to go.

My goal is to transition my clients from being employees of their business to becoming owners of their business. This huge mind shift takes education, awareness and desire. It is my job to help my clients understand the difference between having a job and owning a business, and the critical importance of allowing the business to become a separate entity.

One of the key focuses of my coaching is marketing, which is nothing more than building relationships. I teach my clients that it is about managing relationships from the standpoint of providing support for business development. While it might sound hard, when you know what you are doing, being a business owner can be amazing, exciting and wonderful.

For my clients, working with me is like going on a journey—a journey that leads them to better life balance, to making money even when they are not in the office, and to hiring a functional staff that can maneuver the business using policies and procedures that have been established. I help my clients see the rewards of transforming their clients into raving fans.

I help them gather the strength to develop the independence and ability to make decisions about where they want to take the business, and celebrate with them the feeling of not being at the mercy of someone else's desires and designs. When you walk away from that 9-to-5 grind and build a business that suits your life, it is like having a baby, and when I help my clients get there with their business, I'm like the proud papa.

What lies ahead?

I have earned a reputation as a no-nonsense advisor who knows how to assess issues and create actions that can be immediately implemented for results. My future entails continuing to provide that same level of support in new and vital ways.

Through the training in the SkillPreneur Business System, business owners will gain the knowledge and understanding of how to effectively, efficiently, and profitably run a business to ultimately offer them a better work/life balance.

I have also created this system in such a way that it can be used by other business coaches. To teach coaches how to be a business coach and use the system, I have developed a unique program called Master Business Coach.

Coaches are often SkillPreneurs themselves. The Master Business Coach Program will provide them strategy and support to build a thriving coach practice, as well as the tools to provide knowledge, guidance and support to their own small-business clients. My goal is to help these coaches take a giant leap forward by saving them from the development process of creating their own effective tools, programs and materials, which often take several months and several thousands of dollars to otherwise create.

No matter what the future holds, I know that I will continue to find satisfaction in seeing people transform not only their businesses, but their attitudes about owning a business.

My clients learn the difference between having a job and owning a business. They learn the difference between working in their business and working on their business. And what's really wonderful is that I end up learning as much from them as they learn from me.

My Year of the Phoenix

JUDI RHEE ALLOWAY

Ah, yes! One day you wake up, yawn, wipe the sleep out of your eyes, stretch, roll over in bed, and realize that this day is infinitely different from so many of the 3,650 days preceding. And you think that it could never happen to you…that this is your chance to completely start over …that it's indeed possible to live the life of your dreams.

That is precisely what happened to me on November 19, 2008, as I began my year named for the mythical creature that self-ignites after living five hundred to a thousand years and featured in Indian, Persian, Egyptian, Greek, Russian, Chinese, Japanese, and Catholic legends…as well as a popular Korean drama.

But before I tell you more, let's take a step back…

Open the gates!
"Hey, why is there a line of people waiting to meet us?" I curiously asked as a half-dozen Mongolian civil servants queued in a diagonal line.

For a couple of minutes all of the staff at the Czech embassy in Mongolia had become suspended in time as a line of people waited to greet us. "Oh, you must be the eldest son of A," as they kissed my husband's hand. Then they paused with a smile and turned to me. "And you must be his American wife," as they partially bowed, extending their lips to graze my outreached hand.

An emaciated man with slick, black hair and thick, dark glasses, in a Soviet-inspired gray suit, and who spoke the best Russian, stepped forward to explain the lay of the land, "Welcome to the

Czech embassy. Your two-room apartment is on the second floor with a kitchen, dining room, living room with a TV and international cable featuring American channels, a queen-sized bedroom with plenty of closet space, and a bathroom with a tub. Laundry service is available. Billiards is in the basement where your father often comes. Just let us know what you need."

The staff managed to disperse after this gracious greeting to give us time to explore our new temporary residence in Ulaanbaatar, decorated in the heyday of the Seventies, replete with tangerine velvet couches with bronze touches and a view of auspiciously hanging wolf skins. We were very fortunate to have such a spacious place with electricity, periodic hot water, and gates. Of course, it helped that my husband was the eldest son of A. and I was the "American trophy wife with the Asian face, prized pale skin with peach undertones, and wavy reddish-brown long hair." Basically, I was an oddity for my looks, cleanliness, and dark-blue, gold-embossed passport. My husband's family was well-connected to *buzinesmeni* from Russia, Ukraine, Latvia, and other former Soviet Union countries, and Asia. That made us the normal-looking, Banana Republic-factory-catalogue couple in your local Whole Foods on the weekends in the United States, who were also very well-taken care of when traveling in Asia.

A Bicontinental Divorce

After another visit to Asia to work on our sustainable-agricultural project, deliver donations to a Mongolian orphanage, network with non-governmental organizations (NGOs), and complete the last steps of my birth-family search on KBS-TV, my husband and I had a major falling-out. As the oldest son, he was expected to take over the family business. Our lives were being heading in two different directions. We initially tried to maintain a bi-continental marriage, but we ultimately decided to get a divorce and respect each other's wishes for a "better" life.

There I was on November 19, 2008, pregnant, with a mortgage for a 3-bedroom/$2^{1}/_{2}$-bath home in one of the best neighborhoods in America, some credit-card debt, and without a reliable source of income or medical insurance. I turned to my family for help and ended up taking a line of credit from our credit cards to support and invest in myself. Due to the stress of the situation, I miscarried our child, knowing that there would be another God-given time to have children.

Now, to understand how a simple South Jersey girl ended up marrying into the Mongolian mafia, you need to know a few things about my life before coaching.

> ***Novena to St. Jude:***
> *Oh, sacred heart of Jesus, pray for us.*
> *St. Jude, worker of miracles, pray for us.*
> *St. Jude, helper of the hopeless, pray for us.*
> *Pray nine times a day; by the eighth day your prayers will be answered.*
> *Publication promised.*

I was born from a whisper. Sacred breath birthed my existence, transporting me from Seoul, South Korea, to Tabernacle in South Jersey. I am one of over three hundred thousand adopted Korean orphans who have been spread, like dandelion seeds, across the continents to loving homes since the Korean war of 1950–1953. We became mini-cultural ambassadors, neither belonging to our motherland, nor becoming immediate patriots of our new countries. We are known as OAKs (Overseas Adopted Koreans) and *hangukgye migukin* (Korean-American).

For the first nine months of my life, as a baby ambassador on the reverse time schedule, I sat, watched, and observed the new, strange home in which I had landed, over the rainbow, after the maelstrom of international legal issues. I had one trusty companion that went by his Native-American name, Brownfoot: my beloved beagle. He became my watchdog, ensuring my existence by waking my parents when I was sick from my new diet and when I could not sleep. Then one day, I adjusted to my new life and cracked a smile. My parents remark that I have not stopped smiling since then.

For the next seventeen years, I lived a charmed life in the idyllic ruralburbia close to the Wharton State Forest, equidistant from the Jersey Shore and Philadelphia. Immersed in various experiences academically, in the gifted and talented program academically, outside of school, I played the violin, danced, studied theater, and became captain of numerous sports teams: field hockey, softball, and lacrosse. I even learned Russian at the University of Pennsylvania and appeared on Nickelodeon during middle school. In high school, I was elected vice president of Student Council, was coeditor of the newspaper, was vice president of various clubs that were engaged in environmental, human rights, and international issues, and worked part-time at a retirement home. Yet, something was missing in my seemingly perfect life. Stuck in between the ethnic divide, often experiencing what I perceived to be racism, I struggled, like many others, to find my identity, my calling, and my place in the world.

As you can see, I was a serious over-achiever, and that went on through college and beyond. Suffice it to say that, after acquiring a number of accolades and wonderful experiences, I found myself in the middle of major international events in Washington, DC, and infected with wanderlust. I then left the U.S. to pursue my then-dream of living, traveling, and studying around the world before the age of twenty-five. I ended up in Russia working on my master's degree, researching ideas of world peace through international economic relations at Moscow State University, and found my first taste of freedom from over-achieving. It was at MSU that I met my husband in a Stalinist-functioning elevator after a farewell party with the Europeans on International Women's Day. To continue our international love affair and immigration nightmare, we decided to take the trip of a lifetime and travel with a group of international students, representing six continents, who were on an international mission of peace riding on horseback from Moscow through Kazakhstan to Beijing, to ring in the millennium, which was to be a new era of international cooperation, based on mutual respect and harmony.

Fortunately, my Forrest Gump-like luck slowed down with the economic collapse of Russia. Traveling down south to Slavyansk-na-Kubani, home of the famous Donchiki horses, we discovered that horses made a delicious sausage during times of financial crisis, when salt and not much else could be found on supermarket shelves. We ended up taking the trip by train, stopping in Mongolia, where we "camped" with nomadic relatives in the Gobi Desert and were entertained by members of the mafia onto Beijing. Then I flew to South Korea with $12 in my pocket to study the Korean language at Seoul National University and work as an English-language teacher.

Still, I yearned for a sense of home, purpose, and career. Eventually, I crossed the Pacific, back to the Los Angeles area, to see *The Margaret Cho Show*, and found a job as a financial/tax analyst for a recruiting and career-training firm. After a couple of West Coast earthquakes, I flew back to the East Coast to help take care of my grandmother, who was crippled by rheumatoid arthritis. During this time, we had eloped in secret to live with my Catholic parents and grandmother. Living a clandestine life in an intergenerational home, while my husband began regular trips to "the library as part of his studies at the University of Pennsylvania"— code for *the casinos of Atlantic City*—my only solace was studying yoga and business management. I had decided to pursue the dream I had had at the age of twelve, of working on Wall Street with a briefcase and long straight hair. Although my hair is far from stick straight, I did end up working for a Wall Street firm as a financial advisor involved in event management, marketing, and investment research, in a group catering to "celebrity money" clientele from multicultural Hollywood and national sports teams. In my community, I helped start the Philadelphia Chapter of the National Association of Asian American Professionals and became the professional development chair who created the "Leaders in the Community" series. In my spare time, I freelanced as a bookkeeper for an herbalist and *feng shui* master to help pay for the gorgeous two-story house with a fenced-in backyard that we had bought. My life, once again, seemed perfect.

Healed in the Homeland

That was until the day I woke up with hot, stabbing pains that ravaged my body. As the pains grew, the quality of my life quickly deteriorated as I was shuttled from gynecologist to gastroenterologist to neurologist to more than twelve other "ologists." They all scratched their heads, with no definitive answer. Most commented that I would have to take pain medications and other prescriptions for the rest of my life, in order to keep my body functioning, all the while, as my medical bills amassed. Once a vibrant young community leader, I was now confined to my house and a wheelchair, unable to eat solid foods. I was depressed, frustrated, and yet determined to walk, and even dreamt of running again. We left the U.S. and the American medical system, traveling back to Asia to explore alternative medicine, and that's when I found my calling, as I finally surrendered my life over to the care of the Universe, Spirit, Creator, and God.

When I came back to United States, I walked like a newborn colt and ate some solid foods. For a couple of years, I worked on my own healing through energy, while I started to see clients. I became a spiritual artist and ecstatic poet, and I created a non-profit organization dedicated to "Strength, Love, Peace, and Harmony," serving Mongolian orphans through indigenous wisdom, sustainable agriculture, and community-building. At least that was my life until November 19, 2008, when I woke up to the dawn of a new day.

A New Home in Coaching

Auspiciously, I was already a graduate on the Leadership Committee for New Choices/New Options, a six-week career-training program for single parents, single pregnant women, and displaced homemakers who were interested in non-traditional careers. The program starts with an intensive self-discovery process that culminates in scholarship and financial assistance for further education and other opportunities to fund entrepreneurial endeavors. During the program, I craved to deeply follow my calling to become a life coach, combining my interests of energy, entrepreneurship and service.

At the Leadership Committee meeting, the director of New Choices/New Options informed me that I was eligible for a scholarship to pursue a coach-training program. On that Tuesday, I serendipitously received an email from the Institute for Professional Excellence in Coaching (iPEC), a coach-training program, and Transformations, a holistic learning center, about coach training. The next day, I traveled to Transformations for an event, which was where I met an iPEC coach. I knew, on a spiritual level, that this was my chance to rebuild my life. On Friday of the next week, I started Mod I thanks to being a part of the Economic Hardship Program, and bought my first pair of running shoes, down the street from the coach-training classroom. The day after I finished Mod III, I started working at iPEC as a manager. Daily, I create new ways of reaching out to prospective students and alumni, co-creating the "SHIFT Now!" national movement and events, writing educational articles in the *Coach Community Newsletter*, facilitating the Power of Coaching Presenter Program, and working with an authentic group of coaches who truly care for our prospective students, current students, graduates, and the world beyond coaching.

Named after the patron saint of miracles, I finally have clicked my red, glittery pumps three times and found myself home with

"My life, as you might have guessed, is what it is: perfect!"

extended multicultural families and expansive international communities—my place in the world—taking root in my home of coaching. Coaching has become the forum that allows me to partner and tangibly drill down to polish the gifts and talents that each one of us has to offer the world.

Every day, I have the pleasure of working with many of the contributors to this collaborative work, including Bruce D Schneider, Ed Abel, Raechel Anderson, Jennifer Barley, and Kari Lowrey. I am fortunate to coach and to have been coached by Joseph Amanfu, Anthony Fasano, Samita Loomba, and Michael Reddy, the latter of whom does amazing family constellation work. I am blessed to have met Tim Durling, Ronit Hakimi, Laura Hall, Kilian Kröll, Julie McManus and Kari Lowery, who have become inspirational Power of Coaching Presenters. And hopefully, I'll have a chance to connect with Barbara B. Appelbaum, Deborah Sakelaris, Carol Juergensen Sheets, Jaime Yordan-Frau, and you, curious reader of this book.

And my life, as you might have guessed, is what it is: perfect! When I am not working, I have many hobbies that I enjoy, such as running, doing yoga, dancing, painting, writing, knitting, playing musical instruments, singing, meditating, and praying. I am very lucky to have my physical, emotional, mental and spiritual health and wealth. I am extremely grateful for the rich tapestry of life experiences that I have co-woven with the grace of Divine Will.

Thank you for taking the time to investigate your own interests and dream a new life for yourself, your family and your community.

"Mawusi": In the Hands of God

JOSEPH AMANFU

My life before coaching

I was born and grew up in Ghana, West Africa, as a member of the Ewe tribe. The Ewe language is spoken primarily in the Volta Region of Ghana. Among Ewes, just as in other language groups, there are multitudes of subtle differences in dialect from one town to the next. However, throughout Ghana, there is a common thread of how children are named. Every child enters the world with his or her default first name. The child is named after the day of the week on which he or she was born.

The first names listed here apply specifically to the people in and around Ho, the regional capital of the Volta Region. However, they may apply to other towns and indeed to other Ghanaian language groups. There are several dialectical and tribal variations of these names:

DAY	BOY	GIRL
Sunday	Kwasi (Akwasi)	Akosua (Akoss)
Monday	Kodjo (Kudzo)	Adjoa (Adzo)
Tuesday	Kwamla (Kwabena)	Abra (Abena)
Wednesday	Kwaku (Kweku)	Aku (Ekua)
Thursday	Yao	Yawa (Yaa)
Friday	Kofi	Afua (Efua, Fifi)
Saturday	Kwami	Ama, Ami

The names in parentheses show some of the tribal variations. I can imagine the question going through your mind, right now: "What if we have more than one child of the same sex born in the same household?" Yes, you are right! We have an answer for that dilemma.

We attach a diminutive qualifier after the name. In America, if your name is Joseph and your son is also named Joseph, then your son is called Joseph, Junior. It is the same in Ghana. In my tribe, the term for Junior is either "Fio" or "Kuma" and sometimes, "Tse." My father was born on Wednesday, so his name was "Kwaku." I was also born on Wednesday, so my name is "Kwaku Fio."

Traditionally, if the family goes to church, then the child is baptized around the eighth day and given an English name, normally selected from the Bible. That is how I got my name "Joseph." Some of my American friends still do not believe that we had English names in Africa. They insist that I came up with an English name only when I was coming to America.

It is also customary for the family to give the child a fun personal name. It is often believed that the meaning of this personal name will define the child's destiny. This personal name may be given by the parents, or selected by any loved member of the extended family. My personal name, "Mawusi," was selected by my oldest uncle who lived in Germany for over fifty years. "Mawusi" means "in God's hands." That has truly proved to define my life. God has definitely placed His mighty hands of protection on my life. I believe that nothing will harm me while I am in God's hands.

There is no real limit to the number of names you can write for yourself on official documents in Ghana. So, here is my full name in Ghana:

Joseph Mawusi Kwaku Fio Amanfu

When we were completing our immigration paperwork, to come to the U.S., there was room for only one middle name. I retained my God-given middle name of "Kwaku." Hence, the official name I have on my American documents is Joseph Kwaku Amanfu. I came to the U.S. from Ghana in 1982, with my beautiful wife, Mabel, and three precious children, Edem (Pearl), Eyram (Ruby) and Joe, Jr.

For several years in Ghana, I served as an associate director of the Hour of Visitation Choir and Evangelistic Association

(HOVCEA). I also spent four years with the late Archbishop Dr. Benson Idahosa as an associate pastor of Music of the Redeemed Voices in Benin City, Nigeria. My wife and I completed a two-year Bible School education in the U.S., and have always been actively involved in local churches.

My significant church roots in the States have been: Faith Is the Victory Church in Nashville, TN (under pastor Charles Cowan), Love & Grace Family Church in Omaha, NE (under pastor Dale Marples), Grace Outreach Center in Plano, TX (under pastor Gerald Brooks), and I am currently at New Life Church International in Tallahassee, FL (under pastor Travis Burke).

I have been heavily involved in professional development at the Tallahassee Chapter of the Project Management Institute (PMI), and I am a regular speaker at national and regional PMI events.

During the last eleven years, I enjoyed a very successful career working for Hewlett-Packard. I started as a manager of software engineering, and later, became a senior program manager, managing HP's worldwide telecom projects.

I have spent the past thirty-nine years of my life in the corporate world, during which I completed leadership assignments in Brazil, Canada, Germany, Ghana, Japan, Nigeria, South Africa, Sierra Leone, Thailand, Turkey, and the U.S. I have also been a prolific conference speaker on the subject of leadership development. Most of the materials I use for my conference speaking are taken from the writings of Dr. John C. Maxwell.

While working for Hewlett-Packard, I participated in the company's Mentor-Match program. There was an internal website that contained the profiles of employees who were willing to mentor other employees. HP employees, in any part of the world, who needed a mentor, could review the profiles and select any mentor who was available. For about eight years, I provided remote mentoring to project managers from several countries.

In the early part of 2008, I received an email inviting me to participate in the HP Coaching Network (HPCN). At my first conference call with the HPCN, I asked how coaching differed from the mentoring that I had been doing for many years. Their explanation of the differences encouraged me to find out more about coaching.

After only a few months in the HPCN, there was an announcement of positions open for twelve HPCN candidates to be selected from all over the world to be trained as coaches by Personnel Decisions International (PDI). The trained coaches would be conducting internal 360-degree feedback reviews with other HP employees. After completing my certification training, I provided coaching, via telephone, to several senior engineers and managers.

We had another program within the HPCN called Coaching in the Rounds (CTR). Each CTR participant was assigned a coach and a client. This enabled us to both give and receive peer coaching. My peer coach was in Canada and my peer client was in France.

Once I began to understand more about coaching, I knew this was the field in which I wanted to spend the rest of my life.

My coaching experience so far

During my last three years with Hewlett-Packard, I was assigned, onsite, to a large telecom provider in Johannesburg, South Africa. Those were some of the most enjoyable years of my life. They were also years of growing opportunities, spiritually as well ass maturing through crises in the corporate world. While in South Africa, I saw some billboards promoting life coaches, which gave me the assurance that coaching was indeed recognized worldwide.

In February of 2009, I received the shocking news that my job was eliminated within the Americas. Somehow, I was not surprised, because when I returned at the end of 2008 from my successful, almost three-year assignment in South Africa, my whole team of fifteen employees was gutted and assigned to different managers. The product line that my team supported was no longer profitable in the U.S., even though it was doing extremely well in other countries.

Later, I found out that some of the best engineers and architects I worked with on our specific product line were also laid off. News traveled fast within HP and I received several emails from friends within the company expressing shock and love. The news even got to some of the customers in different countries where I had represented HP. A leader from one of those customers expressed concern that HP did not know what it was doing by letting me go.

One surprising fact was that, just six months earlier, I had been selected as one of the "50 Top Performers" among African-American employees at HP. The fifty of us were brought together in San Diego, CA, for an all-expense-paid African American Leadership Summit. The most senior HP executives were there to acknowledge and speak to us.

Leaving Hewlett-Packard was one of the most difficult decisions I ever made in my life. At almost sixty-one years old, I was at a very major crossroads. I had known, for a few years, that I wanted to focus on my book-publishing and public-speaking businesses, which I had already been doing as a hobby for several years. Deep down inside, I knew that losing my job with HP could be a blessing in disguise for me, but I had wanted to leave on my own terms only after I had put aside an equivalent of at least six months of my salary in an emergency fund. At that time, besides my 401(k) savings, I did not have even one month of my salary in any account.

I received phone calls and emails from France, South Africa and Dubai, offering me leadership positions within HP outside of the U.S.; however, due to my family situation, I could not accept any of the offers to permanently relocate to another country. So, I officially left Hewlett-Packard in April of 2009.

Dr. Bruce D Schneider, founder of the Institute for Professional Excellence in Coaching, said, "Life offers neither problems nor challenges, only opportunities." I am convinced that it is not so much what happens to us, but how we respond to it, that makes the difference in our lives. In the beginning, I struggled with the normal "why me?" syndrome. I communicated with some senior HP executives to try and find out why HP did not give me other assignments within the U.S. I felt that since my primary function was in global project management, I was not tied to any specific product line, and that I could work in any organization within HP. All the senior executives I contacted said that they, too, were scratching their heads about why I was laid off. One of them thought that my salary could be one of the criteria, because I was enjoying a very nice six-figure income. I had to settle on the fact that it was a futile exercise for me to continue trying to understand why.

During the first few weeks after receiving the notice from HP, there was a series of very strange events that convinced me that my decision to leave HP was the right one. Just five days after receiving the layoff notice from HP, an unusual incident happened during church on Sunday morning, February 22, 2009. There was a guest preacher who did not know me from the Man in the Moon. Right in the middle of his sermon, he stopped and walked over to me and said, "Brother, I don't know you, but I feel that God wants me to tell you that He is preparing you for something big. I sense that it is in the area of some business. Get yourself ready! He will be revealing it to you soon."

I shouted back to him, "He has already started! I casually mentioned it to Mom." (I normally address our pastor's wife as "Mom.") I broke down crying. It was clear to me that the Holy Spirit had revealed something to him about me. Later on, towards the end of the service, he came back again and gave me some words of encouragement. By this time, I was sobbing like a baby. Sister Deborah, who was sitting on my left, gave me napkins to wipe away my tears. At the end of the service, I told the preacher and our pastor that the preacher had no idea that God was confirming something of which I was already aware. I said I was not yet ready to discuss the details with anyone.

No one in my family or my church knew that I had received a layoff notice on Tuesday of that week. I printed the large stack of emails and gave them to my wife on Wednesday, and asked her to take some time to read them in detail. I did not give her any idea of how serious the emails were. On Saturday, I asked her if she had read the emails I printed for her and she said, "No." I told her that I was waiting for her to read them before we talked. I decided to wait until she read the emails, which she did several days later.

I was convinced that God wanted me to begin running my own business. When the preacher was speaking to me during the service, he cautioned that God did not want me to do anything stupid. He advised that I needed to carefully pray about the timing.

One part of me said I should get some steady income for a short time while I got ready for my business. This made me think that I should leave all my options open. I seriously thought about some HP management positions open in South Africa and Costa Rica. It was a huge struggle for me to know the difference between God's permissive will and His perfect will.

I requested an appointment for my wife and me to go and discuss this struggle with our pastors. Even after two hours of counseling and prayer, my wife and I did not see clearly what God's perfect will was for us. I had two months to decide whether I was going to remain with HP or leave. In the end, I must confess that it was by default that I just allowed the grace period to expire.

Before leaving HP, I had already become a member of the International Coach Federation (ICF) and had begun searching for schools from which I could get a formal certification as a coach. After a very extensive research, I enrolled with the Institute for Professional Excellence in Coaching (iPEC). By the end of 2009, I had completed all the formal training with iPEC, including its graduate-level certification as an Energy Leadership Index Master Practitioner (ELI-MP).

I am currently based in Tallahassee as a full-time coach, helping people improve their leadership abilities.

We were told during Life Potentials Training that many students develop paying clients before completing their training. I have even spoken with one individual who had twenty-two paying clients before graduating from iPEC. Well, here I am, at the end of 2009, and still do not have even one paying client. Sometimes, I am inclined to be disappointed that I do not yet have any paying clients; however, instead of letting negative thoughts defeat me, I prefer to be like Chinese bamboo.

It is said that during the first four years of planting Chinese bamboo, nothing appears above the ground. It might seem like nothing is happening, but during those four years, the plant is developing an intricate root system. Suddenly, during the fifth year, that bamboo suddenly shoots from almost nothing to about eighty feet high.

I know that I am building my root system right now. I have provided many coaching sessions as a professional courtesy. The following list shows just a few of my clients:

An old high-school mate with a PH.D. degree, who is now a college professor in the U.S.;

An American gentleman who is the director of an international leadership school;

A director of finance for one of the departments in the Florida government;

A married couple who are the pastors of a church;

A regular weekly client in Ghana, who is the founder and president of a company with several employees.

Instead of giving in to the fear of running out of money, I will continue to remain faithful to my mission of becoming one of the best and most highly sought-after coaches in the world. I remember a verse in the Bible that says, "A faithful man will be richly blessed." (*Proverbs* 28:20)

This scripture tells me that committed and persistent work pays off, and that get-rich-quick schemes are ripoffs. I intend to be richly blessed as I continue to be a blessing to others. Motivational speaker Zig Ziglar said that if you help enough people get what they want in life, they will, in turn, help you get what you want.

One of the iPEC processes, from which I have benefitted most, is that we were assigned peer coaches, peer clients and peer coaching groups. We were also assigned to mentor coaches who are former iPEC graduates. My weekly telephone sessions with each of these people have given me tremendous growth. We also participated in weekly teleclasses that discussed topics that have turned me into a more confident individual. The knowledge I have gained from my involvement with iPEC is literally transforming my life.

In the meantime, I am not just sitting down and waiting for things to happen. I am doing a lot of reading and participating in community activities. One of the most helpful ones is the Tallahassee Chamber of Commerce. In addition to the network of business-development resources, there are several small groups called Leads Groups. Each Leads Group has membership room for only one person from each different industry or field of work. These groups meet once a week to build relationships and exchange ideas about how to help one another's business through referrals.

Before settling in my current Chamber of Commerce Leads Group, I took several weeks and visited each one to evaluate how it conducted business. Even though each group has its unique strengths, I had to choose the one that I felt best met my aspirations and community style. The group that I joined is a very lively and almost rambunctious club. The meaning of the word rambunctious, according to the *Encarta Dictionary* is "noisy, very active, and hard to control, usually as a result of excitement or youthful energy." The author of the entry must have visited my Leads Group sometime in the past. I also recently joined a local Chapter of Business Network International (BNI).

Where I see myself going with my coaching business
One of my biggest struggles, after the initial iPEC training class, was determining which area of coaching I wanted to focus on. They asked us to decide on our niche area. I do not remember ever hearing or seeing the word *niche* until I started training with iPEC. Okay, I might have heard the word sometime in my life, but never paid attention to it. It is defined in *Webster's Online Dictionary* as, "A position particularly well suited to the person who occupies it. Example: *'He found his niche in the academic world.'* "

I also found the following interesting definitions of the word *niche* in the *Encarta Online Dictionary*:

> **1. suitable place for somebody:** a position or activity that particularly suits somebody's talents and personality or that somebody can make his or her own.
>
> *She carved out her own niche in the industry.*
>
> **2. COMMERCE specialized market:** an area of the market specializing in one type of product or service.

designed to undercut the competition in the same niche

3. ECOLOGY **place in nature:** the role of an organism within its natural environment that determines its relations with other organisms and ensures its survival.

The key words I found in all these definitions are "personality," "talents," and "well-suited." It was difficult for me to decide on the position that was well-suited to my talents, personality and passion. In one sense, as a result of my thirty-nine years of success in the corporate world, I felt that I could be useful in coaching the corporate world. On the other hand, I have been very heavily involved in the church and Christian organizations almost all my life. Therefore, I felt that I could relate better to Christians, and provide coaching, especially to those who are lazy and just sit down expecting God to drop manna from heaven, cook it and lay it on their dinner tables.

As part of our coach training at iPEC, we were given several books to read. One of the books was *Book Yourself Solid* by Michael Port. In his book, he devotes a whole chapter to "Developing a Personal Brand." He quoted the following statement:

> "Every time you suppress some part of yourself or allow others to play you small, you are in essence ignoring the owner's manual your creator gave you and destroying your design." —Oprah Winfrey

Michael Port includes several exercises in his book and I took them very seriously. One of the exercises taught me how to develop my target market and my "Elevator Speech." I decided that if anyone ever asked me, "What kind of work do you do?" I would provide the following long-winded response:

> "You know how young people, between twenty-five and forty years old, want to have significance in life, make money and live a happy life? Well, what I do is help them identify who they are on the inside, and what their life purpose is. I help them solidify the reasons they want what they want, give them encouragement and affirmations about the talents and gifts they

already have, and help them discover endless options that they had not seen or even imagined before. The ultimate benefit is that they become more excited in life."

I memorized the above response and even tried it out a few times. Frankly, when I look at that response today, I realize how little I knew in the beginning. I wonder how many people have the time to listen to a lecture when they ask a simple question, "What kind of work do you do?"

Even though I had decided on my target market or niche group, I still had some reservations on the inside as to whether I had made the right choice. During one of our iPEC teleclasses, I explained my dilemma to Bruce Schneider. He encouraged me to consider focusing on the corporate world as a business coach. I felt that he must have noticed something about me that I did not clearly see. I tend to listen to the wisdom of people who have been successful in their fields. So, I made the decision to call myself a business coach.

My trepidation did not end there. I still had some self-doubt about my success as a business coach in America. I was blessed to have a wonderful peer coach who helped me through all these struggles. During one of our coaching sessions, I explained to her that I was not sure American society would embrace someone like me, having grown up in Africa. I told her that I thought part of the reason for my outstanding success in the corporate world was that I was working under the umbrella of the mighty Hewlett-Packard Company.

Now that I am running my own coaching business, I felt that, when I talk to people, my accent might be a handicap and liability. She observed that, from her perspective, my accent was one of my greatest assets because anytime she heard me speak, she was genuinely interested in hearing about my life. She said people would also be more interested in listening to me because of my extensive global corporate experience.

It is very interesting to note how we limit ourselves with negative self-talk. I should have remembered that, anytime I spoke at a conference anywhere in the world, people came to me afterwards and commended me on my English and my pace of speaking. Why should I now be limiting myself by something that has worked so well in the past?

I owe a great debt of gratitude to my peer coach, Lynn Ely, for helping me realize the advantage that I have, even as a foreigner. She told me that I am living proof of the American Dream and

> *"It is very interesting to note how we limit ourselves with negative self-talk."*

that I need to emphasize my global experience. This empowered me to change my introduction. From that time onwards, when I introduced myself at my Chamber of Commerce Leads Group and other public meetings, the following was what I said:

> "My name is Joseph Amanfu. I am living proof of the American Dream, a business coach with extensive global experience and thirty-nine years in the corporate world. For the past eleven years, I managed HP's (Hewlett-Packard's) worldwide telecom projects. I am now equipped as a certified business coach, helping businesses improve their people and their performance."

Anytime I sent out an email, the following variation was quoted under my email signature:

> "Dr. Amanfu is living proof the American Dream. A Certified Life & Business Coach with extensive global experience. Thirty-eight years in the corporate world, with the last eleven years managing HP's (Hewlett-Packard's) worldwide telecom projects. Completed leadership assignments in Brazil, Canada, Germany, Ghana, Japan, Nigeria, Sierra Leone, South Africa, Thailand, Turkey and the U.S.A. Currently based in Tallahassee as a full-time business coach, helping businesses improve their people and their performance. He is also a prolific conference speaker on the subject

of leadership development."

I must add that my training as a coach is not only preparing me to help others improve their lives and businesses; my own life is being transformed in a very positive way. I am now more conscious of myself, my words, my actions and even my thoughts. I heard Bruce Schneider explain that we must *be* coaches and not *do* coaching. I now realize that I am always a coach. I do not practice coaching—I *am* a coach.

To illustrate how much I have grown within this short period of time, I want to share the following episode with you. It occurred only this morning, the day that I am writing this section of my story.

There is a young lady in America who often asks for my advice on different matters. I need to point out that I am a very close friend of her husband and she normally calls me "Dad." This morning, while I was doing my walking exercise, she called me on the phone and said, "Dad, I need you to listen to this statement and tell me if it makes sense." She said she was struggling with writing a certain statement about her business and so she requested her attorney to rewrite it for her. She said what her attorney wrote "does not make sense." She read the information to me on the phone; it contained about three sentences. Then she asked, "Dad, that does not make sense, does it?"

Prior to my coach training, I might have told her right away what I thought. Instead, I asked her, "What part of it does not make sense?" She was startled by my question. I explained that I was not saying it *did* make sense; I just wanted her to tell me which parts did not make sense to her. To my surprise, she read the first sentence and said that part was okay. Then, she read the second sentence and, again, said that part was okay. Then, she read the last sentence and asked, "Dad, that does not make sense, does it?"

I was in my coaching mode at its best. It sounded to me that all she wanted was for me to agree with her. After a lengthy back-and-forth between us, as she kept pushing, I said to her, "I am a coach, and so I am not supposed to tell you what to do." She rudely interrupted me, her voice sounding very emotional, and said, "I don't need a coach right now. All I need is someone to listen to me and tell me if what the attorney wrote makes sense."

I felt like telling her, "Listen, young lady, I am a coach. So if you do not want a coach, then please don't ever ask me for advice in the future." Instead, I kept my cool and allowed her to talk herself out, after which I said, "Goodbye." This episode reveals to me how much I have changed.

Selected testimonials

It is very fulfilling for me to know that I am making a difference in the lives of many people. Following are a few selected testimonials, printed with special permission from my clients.

From SH, a business owner. I have been providing weekly coaching to SH for several weeks now. For the past two sessions, he was not available due to some challenges. He was sensing that I was disappointed and was afraid that I might be dropping him as a client.

> I perceived you're a very busy person and your schedules are very tight but you had time to help me. Unfortunately I've not been able to help myself in order to appreciate your commitment towards me especially for the past few weeks. I'm struggling to make amends with life and my future and I always believe you're God-sent to help but in as much as I tried, my problems are just unfolding and I'm finding it very difficult to cope. I couldn't figure out what I was doing wrong until you came into my life. Please don't give up on me otherwise I cannot survive the next time around. I know I'm born to be great but "HOW?" is what I cannot understand. Please don't give up on me. I'll do everything possible to help myself if you're ready to support me as you've already started but kindly understand where I'm coming from. I told you part of my story on phone and I hope you can imagine someone like me trying on his own by the grace of God to make ends meet in this geographical location where help only comes from God. The environment here has not been conducive for certain people to make it possible. Society finds it difficult to understand certain conditions of people. Maybe they think it's our destiny. Please, I'm ready to prove them wrong. I'm of age but lack some experience. Since I met you online (spiritually) I believe God is helping me make amends. It is NOT over with me until its OVER!
>
> My observers will see what God can do through and for me. My mental problem is hindering me so much but God is helping me one day at a time. As I'm sending you this mes-

sage tears are rolling down from my eyes because I know God has a plan for me and I'll not let HIM nor you down.

All I'm asking for is time and good health. I've been dispirited and ignored by many people I counted on even at times but my wife and I don't blame them. My children always love me just as I am. They cannot see any difference, all they know is that I'm still and always their father. They are my only joy and comfort!

Please call me on Monday as usual and let's continue our lessons. Forget about my workers as of now. By the grace of God I'll inspire them from what I've studied from you. It is my duty to make people see what and who I am.

My first achievement I owe to you is that I was selected as the Organizing Secretary to the Men's Fraternity of my church. Thank God I'm learning to grow! Please continue to pray for me, I need prayers, I need God at all times. Keep this message in memory of me. You'll be proud of me one day!

Have a great day and may God be with you.

—SH

Sometimes, it becomes necessary to be extra-firm in dealing with clients who do not seem to be fulfilling their end of the bargain. In order to be helpful to my clients, I have often had the need to confront them openly. The following example is an excerpt from an email I sent to one of my clients. This gentleman is the president of a very-high-profile organization and is also pursuing his doctoral studies, at the same time. I sensed that he had not fully decided to devote his time to our coaching relationship.

"...The conclusion I came to was that you probably have too much going on in your life at the moment and that you might not have time to devote to a coaching relationship. Coaching is a very serious work and can bring tremendous results to anyone's life. But it requires dedication. I'm sure you know that I am extremely busy, and I know that you are busy too. But if you can truly devote one hour every 2 weeks, then I will be glad to re-schedule."

As far as my future is concerned, I believe that God has a special assignment for me in the church world. I will keep my ears, my heart and my mind open to listen to where God leads me. Where He leads me, I will follow.

My inclination, at this point, is that I will end up focusing on leadership coaching, especially within the church world. We discovered, during our coach training, that each of us has his/her own Higher Coach. As coaches, we are not judgmental of others and their choices.

As a Christian, I know that my Higher Coach is the Almighty God, Himself. I believe that my Higher Coach lives inside me and I give Him first place in my life; however, I do not use my beliefs as the basis of coaching my clients. I primarily depend on the coaching process itself and my coaching skills. I never even tell my clients who my Higher Coach is. Coaching is all about the client and not at all about the coach.

One of the techniques we were taught during coach training is "centering." This is a process of calming oneself down and regaining focus. In addition to the powerful techniques I learned, I also use different passages of scripture for quick, personal centering depending on the situation. I use different scriptures when I am afraid; when I face financial challenges; when I am angry; when I need more peace in my life; and when I am sad.

Because of what Jeremiah 29:11 tells me, I am convinced that God has great things in store for me. I want to dedicate the rest of my life to planting seeds of hope and changing lives.

Breaking through the Bipolar Disorder Ceiling

JOURNEY

4

RAECHEL ANDERSON

On March 21, 2003, I was diagnosed with Type I bipolar disorder. A series of devastating experiences had occurred over the course of the two years prior and the ramifications of those events had sent me spiraling to rock bottom and, thus, dumped me in the office of that psychiatrist, on that day. As I sat in the doctor's office listening to the diagnosis and details about my disorder, I immediately began to mourn the death of my life pursuits, at the mere age of twenty-five. I was truly relieved to finally have an explanation for the many irrational behaviors that I had exhibited over the last couple of years, but I was realizing that, between the lifelong consequences of the poor decisions that I had made and my now named mental illness, the goals and dreams that I had were no longer possible.

At that time, I was attending law school, with the end goal of being a high-powered, well-respected member of the bar and, eventually, a renowned jurist. That was no longer possible. No one would hire a manic-depressive lawyer—much less elect or appoint one to a judicial role. Why bother continuing law school? So, I dropped out of law school immediately.

I was the business manager at a law firm at that time. Thus far, I had invested six years of my life into the business and corporate world, with the intention of working from the ground up as part of yet another long-term goal, which was to experience and fully appreciate all aspects of leadership and management in business. It was my intention to eventually use these experiences to start my own business—a law firm—and, perhaps, even represent other businesses. So, since I was neither going to be a lawyer, nor would I have my own practice to run, and. since no one would want to do business or work for someone who was bipolar, why keep working? So, I quit my job.

So, there I was: no job, no career, no future, and—most important—no hope.

After a few weeks, I had accepted my demise and decided that I had nothing to lose by following the treatment plan my doctor suggested. Over the course of the next six to eight months, by following the treatment plan, my psychosis departed and my anxiety diminished. My moods stabilized and the fog started to lift. After another six months, I still didn't believe there was much hope, but my desire to have some kind of life returned. I didn't know where to start or what would work, but I knew I was ready to try something. I also knew that, no matter what I did, it would be difficult, and I would have to really labor to accomplish anything significant. At that point, I was determined to do that.

I came bursting out of the box, full-force, jumping back into life. I worked quickly and avidly to bandaid my mistakes and errors in all aspects of life: relationships, career, health, etc. I had accepted that I wasn't going to be a lawyer, which was fine with me, but I could still do life again without a legal career. So, I delved back into the business world. I sought out and was hired for a low-level, low-paying job, which, of course, was the best that I could do given my condition. I knew the days when I could manage others were long gone.

Most of my immediate, impulsive attempts to retake life were not successful or sustainable. This wasn't due to the fact that I didn't want them to be; I did. It probably had something to do with the lack of thought and awareness behind the actions. The good news was that I wasn't giving up, and I was refusing to live under a rock; the bad news: I would have to continue to flounder around until I found what I needed, because I had no direction or example to follow. I knew of no one else in my situation who was functioning well, and many who were far worse. At the end of the day, I wasn't happy, and felt totally incomplete in nearly every way, but I was back in life, at least as much as I could ever be. After all, I did live beneath the glass ceiling of bipolar disorder, always looking up to see the success of others, and knowing that I could never go that far.

After a year of fighting those battles—the results of which, I was beginning to realize, weren't much better than the barely existing life that I had lived the prior year—a series of events happened during the first half of 2005 that caused me to have a *huge* realization: "My life isn't over!" Yes, I have a serious mental illness, but I can still accomplish great things. No, maybe not the same great things as before and probably not really extraordinary things—but still, I can do some great stuff!

I quit my job and started a consulting company with a couple of other individuals. I applied to a business administration master's program, and was accepted. I also started to really appreciate the importance of helping others who were in the same situation as me. I started doing research about mental illness and sought out organizations that advocate for and support the mentally ill. I came across NAMI, the National Alliance on Mental Illness, and joined their speaker's circuit, so that I could offer my help to others.

Over the course of the next couple of years, I started to live life again—on a much more real level. I had some successes, and I had some failures. I repaired some relationships, and accepted that others might never be healed. I formed new bonds and friendships, and let some others go. I was amazed by the success of my career as a consultant, and I started to believe that I was capable of being a successful businesswoman, even given my limitations. At that time, I perceived this period of my life as a rehabilitation of me as a person and of my past mistakes. I continued to encounter struggles in many areas of my life. Some I worked through; some I accepted would always be. I became at peace with the limitations of my mental illness.

In August of 2007, I turned thirty years old and it was in the celebration of that milestone that I became acutely aware of a feeling of emptiness inside. I really questioned that, because I thought I had everything I could have: a loving husband, a close family, great friends, a career I was good at, and much more. Upon reflection, what I discovered I was missing was a sense of accomplishment, completion, and joy; however, I had no idea where to go to find that sense of fulfillment or joy. What else could I do, given the inherent limitations of my mental illness?

So, I started polling others and exploring the Internet for ideas. I have no idea how, but I stumbled across the concept of life coaching. I was intrigued by the idea—mostly because I knew of no one out there who did it, so it was unique and fascinating, and I wasn't able to place my own biases on it. Coaching seemed a little like what I did as a consultant, but it was also about partnering with and helping others, especially those in rough situations. That really resonated with me.

I did some research and contacted a life coach in the next town over. She offered to have a conversation about coaching and, during that chat, she mentioned the training that she had at iPEC. I got off the phone and went to iPEC's website. I was immediately engaged, and I knew I wanted to do the training to boost the skills I already had, to make me even more successful as a consultant; however, I wasn't ready to take the step at that time. I had way too many other demands on my time. Besides, I had a lifetime to perfect my consulting skills.

A few months later, in January of 2008, I was sitting in the capstone class of my MBA program. This was my last class and its purpose was to synthesize and actualize all that we had just learned over the past few years. The primary method of doing so was to run a simulation that would take place over the four months of the class. We were divided up into teams with each team forming a separate business. The goal of the simulation was to implement all of our learned skills to ensure our business turned in the highest profit possible. The team with the highest profit at the end of the semester would win fabulous prizes—I was in!

I was in a group with three of my best friends, all of us had real-life experiences that spanned the needs of a modern business. Still, two weeks into the simulation, we were in last place, and bleeding red in the profit-and-loss column. We were in a situation where we had to sacrifice a significant amount of human resources and lay off multitudes of employees to turn a profit. It was at that moment that something totally unexpected hit me: *I didn't want to work with corporations anymore.* I didn't want to play the corporate game anymore. I was tired of it being all about the bottom line and not about the employees and human element of the corporation. I realized that my values placed people ahead of turning a profit, and I decided, at that moment, that I was going to honor that, at all costs, starting immediately. Right then, in class, I stopped my work on the simulation and looked at my three friends and said, "I am going to be a life coach." What shocked me most was that not one of them was surprised. They all smiled and one even said, "Yeah, that sounds about right."

I went home, and, as soon as I found my husband, declared, "I've figured out what I want to be when I grow up!" He turned around, and looked at me, and said, quizzically, "A consultant?" I said, "Nope, a life coach." He went back to his work chuckling, but not surprised, and already completely supportive. The next day, I called iPEC, and signed up to start in the November class, to be known as Chicago 15. I knew this would change my life, but I had no idea just how much it would!

On November 7th of the same year, I showed up for my first day of coach training, at Life Potentials Training, prepared for another round of schooling. I walked out of class, on November 9th, an entirely different person. That weekend awakened me to life; it awakened me to freedom; it awakened me to all that I was missing; but—most importantly—it awakened me to *me*.

Through all the amazing exercises and training that weekend, I became completely and totally aware of the fact that I had become my illness, and I had allowed it to label me, block me, and limit me. I had decided—without any real basis—that I could not live the life I wanted. That I could not be the person that I wanted to be. That I could not have the career I wanted. That I could not be as happy as I had dreamed of being. I also became very aware that I had convinced myself that I was living the life I truly wanted to live and, yet, I really wasn't living.

Needless to say, in November 2008, my life changed forever, and for good. I am not now, nor will I ever be, again, the person I was back then and live that life again. The balance of my coach training opened my eyes, mind, and heart to the endless possibilities for all things. I see the world from a different perspective. I have altered the words I use to create a more empowering envi-

ronment for myself and others. I look for opportunities in everything, even in the most difficult situations.

My insecurities have waned. My relationships with everyone
have been permanently impacted for the better. I've been able to
accomplish things I never thought I could. On top of that, I got
to experience all of this with 19 other dear friends, and because of
that, I have developed an amazing support system. More than
anything, this training has given me freedom, that is, the freedom
from the limiting beliefs that held me back and blocked me in
every aspect of life.

Since attending the Energy Leadership training in Boston, in

"I am now living the life of unlimited potential!
Scratch that... I am unlimited potential!"

May of 2009, life is leaps and bounds more exhilarating than before!

I've founded "The W.A.Y. Coaching" and chosen to specialize
in coaching two very distinct groups of people: brides planning a
wedding and those who are affected by mental illness. While they
are two vastly different types of clients, my passion for coaching
both stems out of passions that I have, such as excellence, satisfaction in any success, big-picture and perspective mastery, empathy and understanding for the mentally ill and their families, and
moving forward, "regardless."

I've created an innovative "Wedding According to You" coaching system that helps brides have a fabulous wedding experience
by partnering with them to learn and implement new skills, concepts, and habits that eliminate stress, reduce communication and
relationship strain, and allow them to create the wedding they
truly want.

Additionally, I am now an inspirational speaker on mental illness, both for NAMI and for other groups. I have the opportunity to draw on my own personal experience when I speak and relate to a variety of audiences, such as students of psychology and
psychiatry in undergraduate, graduate, and medical schools;
physicians and psychiatrists; mental illness support groups; fami-

ly and church groups; and the patients in local psychiatric units. I've defined one of my life purposes as being an intentional part of the eradication of the stigma attached to mental illness.

I've gone back to volunteer at every Life Potentials Training and Energy Leadership Training that takes place in Chicago. The exhilaration that comes with that experience does amazing things for me, each time, and, having the opportunity to watch others experience the same thing, is truly a blessing.

So, if you were to ask me to tell you what iPEC has done for me in one sentence, here it is: "I am now living the life of unlimited potential!"

Wait...scratch that.

"I *am* unlimited potential!"

Facing Adversity: Discovering a Gift

Barbara B. Appelbaum

My life prior to coaching

It was a day like any other. I was sitting at my desk, working on a proposal for funding, with a hot cup of coffee at my side. My staff was running in and out of my office with a slew of panicked questions regarding whatever crisis was currently at hand. It was 11:15 a.m. on Thursday, April 26, 2006. Amidst this normal chaos, I noticed my right hand was getting that prickly feeling that quickly precedes numbness when I'm getting a migraine. I took my medication and waited for the sensation to subside. When it hadn't an hour later, I took more medication. The migraine never developed, yet the numbness in my hand never subsided.

Over the weekend, I had a friend visiting from out of town. Our entire time was disrupted by my discomfort with the numbness in my hand. At breakfast on Sunday, I thought my food tasted like tin. My friend said the food was fine and thought I was acting silly. It was then that I realized the entire right side of my body, including the inside of my mouth, was numb. I had also lost partial vision in my left eye. Something was seriously wrong! "My God, I've had a stroke!" Or at least, that's what I thought, based on the symptoms. I was terrified.

The next three weeks were a whirlwind of uncomfortable tests, doctors' hypotheses (stroke, brain tumor, etc.), and expressions of concern from my family and coworkers. In the end, the dreaded words were uttered by the specialist at the University of Chicago Medical Center, "My dear, beyond a shadow of a doubt, you have multiple sclerosis." *Did I hear the doctor correctly? Did I really have*

41

some illness that would never go away? Could I not be cured with a pill or surgery? After forty-seven years, how had my life come to this? Was I going to die? Panic began to eat at my insides as I tuned out all conversation around me.

Decisions had to be made and medications selected. My chosen protocol was injecting beta-interferon, every other day, for the rest of my life, unless scientific research came up with a better alternative. There was only one thing to do: make it my job to learn how to care for myself so my life would not skip a beat. Permission to be "sick" was not an option I was going to allow myself.

I called a psychologist friend and requested two hours of his time, because I was in crisis, and needed to know if there were tricks to handling it all. During this visit, he gave me a newsletter that was all about living with a chronic illness. That newsletter changed my life dramatically. It talked about considering this illness as a "gift." Gifts come in strange forms and our job in life is to recognize them and make them our own.

Within a year of being diagnosed, new leadership came on board at work, and I was laid off from my position as Senior Director of Development. This happened after five years of my commitment, hard work, and proven results to the Foundation (one of six entities of a hospital system in suburban Chicago). At first, I was surprised, then angry, and finally relieved. For the past year, I had been treated like someone who was sick, though I had missed only five days of work during the entire time my personal health was in jeopardy, and I never once complained to colleagues about my health status. In the end, I realized the overall stress of working in a toxic, negative environment was not conducive to my staying healthy. So, in the form of a layoff, another "gift" presented itself to me.

What led me to coaching?

What does one do when unemployed? Network, network, network! I was blessed that the majority of the donors, with whom I had worked, stepped up to the plate with offers of assistance as I began my journey into self-discovery. It is important to note here that I never planned on a career in fundraising and nonprofit. It found *me* because I was good at it, not because I wanted to do it. During those years, I had never really thought about what I truly wanted to do with my life because it never seemed an option. Now, I had that chance, and I was going to take full advantage of the opportunity.

After months of talking to people in the healthcare arena, the vocation of life coaching started to frequently come up in conversation. Then, at an investment meeting, I sat next to a corporate coach who encouraged me to research the industry. She felt I had

"What does one do when unemployed? Network, network, network!"

the right personality, education, and empathy for the profession. The thought of transforming lives and making a difference, every day, that positively impacted people, really resonated with me.

This made sense because I was raised with the notion that we are all here on this earth to make a difference for the better. As my father always says, "Cast bread upon the water and it comes back chocolate cake!" A spark was ignited deep inside me. My passion for health and wellness finally had a means of expression.

What has the iPEC training done in and through my life?

Upon researching the International Coach Federation (ICF), I soon discovered the Institute for Professional Excellence in Coaching (iPEC). iPEC's Core Energy Coaching™ process, Energy Leadership Index training, business-development mentor program, and ongoing support system are what prompted me to choose iPEC for my professional training.

Through iPEC, I have taken a unique journey. The friendships formed are bonds that will never fade and that I will cherish forever. Personally, I have grown tremendously, and learned how to use my strengths in order to help people live up to their own potential and, even, exceed it at times. I have always known that living a balanced life with a mind–body–spirit connection leads to wellness in every aspect, and I found it refreshing that iPEC reinforces that notion throughout its training. It has taught me how to create personal and financial freedom, which is essential for me in managing my own health. Wanting to share my gift with others so that they, too, can live a more fulfilling life, is something the training at iPEC has also afforded me the opportunity to do. Its comprehensive training and mentoring throughout the entire journey have been invaluable. The lifelong support it offers is priceless.

On a very personal note, iPEC also reinforced in me the belief of *I AM*, meaning how we define ourselves without excuses, limiting beliefs, or false assumptions. The reason this is so significant to me is that my MS medic-alert bracelet has engraved on one side, "I AM Living in Wellness," along with the Hebrew letters representing "I AM." This symbolizes the healing prayer I have practiced for over two years with a rabbi focusing on my relationship with God and my thankfulness to Him for keeping me well. iPEC and I shared similar thinking before I even knew iPEC existed!

Where do I see my coaching business in the future?

My vision for my coaching business is vast. The niche I have chosen is wellness (if you haven't guessed by now). My target market is those over forty years old who are facing the second half of their lives. My goal is to provide them with a method to improve and, perhaps, protect their quality of life, so as to live in the moment and enjoy wellness in every aspect of their lives. With over twenry-three years' work experience—twelve of which were in the nonprofit healthcare sector, as well as my personal passion for wellness—I believe I can help people become active participants in their life, health and wellness.

That being said, I recently formed Appelbaum Wellness LLC. Services provided include:

> Coaching to help replace unhealthy behaviors with beneficial ones;
>
> Partnering with clients to write a business plan for their personal lives;
>
> Offering the ELI (Energy Leadership Index) assess-

ment, debrief and client workbook;

Creating a vision board for the year ahead to stay focused on and inspired by one's goals and desires;

Offering tools to navigating personal healthcare (e.g., questions for the doctor, understanding the system, "what to do if" to avoid unnecessary stress);

Proving that small sustainable choices lead to remarkable changes.™

Appelbaum Wellness LLC offers individual life and small-business coaching, Energy Leadership Index assessments, and a variety of workshops. Please visit our website to begin your personal wellness journey and learn to "Live in Wellness Now."™ www.appelbaumwellness.com

Now that you have read this chapter, you may be asking yourself, "So what did I learn from all of this?" A line from my favorite poem sums it up: "Birth is a beginning, death a destination…and life is a journey…"

The key in life is to enjoy the journey and live in the moment. As coaching and iPEC have taught me, release yourself from what happened yesterday; face today and tomorrow with a positive attitude; and, if you just allow life to be, you will experience high energy, joy and fulfillment. And who wouldn't want that?

From High Tech to Life Tech

JENNIFER BARLEY

I remember it clearly. I was sitting in a conference room that was appropriately named after a popular, local surfing spot. There were ten, or so, of us around the long, oval table—feeling oh-so-official. The discussion was intense. It had been hours—back and forth, back and forth—"Well, what do you think?" "Here are the pros and here are the cons." "This is extremely important—we need to make sure not to mess this up." And around it went.

The question of the day was: "Should our software be Java x.xx certified or the later release of x.x? I did not give an x.x rat's ass about the whole discussion.

Here it was, a beautiful summer day in downtown Santa Cruz, and I was wasting hour after hour in discussions and debates over a topic about which I did not care one way or the other.

That afternoon, I went into my cubicle, opened up a spreadsheet, and began entering my husband's and my finances: bills, salary, etc. That was the moment I began figuring out my high-tech exit strategy.

After twelve years of the Silicon Valley high-technology industry—and not all bad, mind you—I was ready to leave. I had met amazing people, worked on cutting-edge projects, earned a good living, and felt like "someone." The other side was 70-hour work-weeks, projects I didn't care about, long commutes, usually working outside my home town, and, mainly, not a connection for me. *Who am I?*

I went home that afternoon and talked to my husband, showed him the spreadsheet, and told him I was ready to quit my job. He asked, "What will you do?" I responded, "I want to find my passion. Until that happens, I want to get closer to my community." After a few more questions, Curtis said, "Go for it!" He always does.

Within two weeks, I quit my job and got a gig slinging eggs at the local breakfast joint. I met school teachers, firemen, carpenters, harbormasters, housewives and real estate agents—all people who lived and worked in my community. I was happy.

During the next fourteen months, I really searched for my pas-

"What made me tick?
What was I connected to?"

sion. *What made me tick? What was I connected to? What would make a difference in people's lives? What would make a difference in my life?* I headed down the path of interior design.

During this process, thanks to "mistakes" at the restaurant—and, well, just eating too much—I gained some weight and joined Weight Watchers. I lost forty pounds and decided to become a Weight Watcher Leader while pursuing interior-design courses.

Leading Weight Watchers meetings, helping people by inspiring them to lose weight, was amazing. I loved it! To see people change their lives and create the life they choose was truly empowering. After a few years of the group environment, I knew my true passion: I decided to become a life coach.

I spent some time thinking about it, investigating schools, and wondering whether that was the right decision. I had put a lot of time, effort and money into the interior-design route. Then came the day that changed my life. I was getting ready to lead a Weight Watchers meeting and a member came up to me to ask: "Are you a Life Coach? I so need a life coach and if you are one, I want to hire you." 'Nuff said!

I researched schools, programs, the International Coach Federation, and selected iPEC (Institute for Professional Excellence in Coaching); I became a certified professional coach. I now have a full coaching business, and I am a lead instructor with iPEC.

My personal mission statement and belief share the idea that anyone can create any life he or she chooses. I get to live out that purpose every day and moment in my life. I live out that mission by "coaching myself up" with understanding and identifying my own choices, working with clients one-on-one, and teaching students to go out and spread the message.

Internal happiness and joy fill my life, and that is because I created the life I chose.

Team Olivia

Stephanie Davis

Through the darkness

This is the story of a personal journey through one woman's fight to save her daughter, lead her family, and find strength and hope along the way.

She's lying in the Pediatric Intensive Care Unit (PICU) now. Her head is bandaged; her body still. The sights and sounds of the ward are familiar. Machines are clicking, beeping, whirling, and lights are flashing. It is busy! Many sick children today, and my daughter is among them, again.

I remember the first time we were here. My skin crawled every time I walked into the ward; the smell of antiseptic, the stiff cold air, traumatized parents, and many distraught grandparents. Death! Yes, sometimes it felt like death. It was a feeling that rocked me deeply. The ones I prayed more for, the parents I watched more than others; the ones I worried for most; some trying to detach to save their hearts, others crashing and letting it all out. I remember thinking that PICU was the darkest and saddest place I had ever seen. Back then, it was too hard to comprehend that we were a part of this seemingly sick, sick world.

I see things differently now. Today, I watch in awe at the amazing team of nurses interacting seamlessly to provide medication, treatment and attention to each child in a bed. I watch a grandmother reading the Bible and explaining each verse to her grandchild. I see a couple in the corner embrace and hold each other for a very, very long time. They seem to be amazed watching their child breathe—slowly breathing in and out, in and out. They have hope. I can see it on their faces; I hear it in their voices. Their child is breathing. That seems to be enough right now. Tonight, she is breathing and living, and they are happy. They have hope.

I reach into my bag and carefully withdraw the old worn-out journal that's been my constant companion for a very long time. I find comfort in reflecting on our journey; seeing how far we've come; seeing how our lives have changed, how love and hope have seen us through. I settle back into the soft leather chair next to Olivia's bed and slowly turn the page.

I never thought that woman would be me. I never expected to be the one whose life was drastically and unexpectedly changed—forever. This journey I'm on, the one I'm leading, seems like a dream: very surreal, like it can't really be happening. At least, not to me. At least, not to my family. Especially not to my sweet Olivia. But I'm snapped back to reality every day, every moment, no matter how much I long to wake up and have life make sense again. I've decided that sense should be left to someone else, because in my new world, there is no logic, there is no sense, but I have found there can be hope.

Before I explain how the coaching process has helped me deal with a very personal, very tragic family crisis, I need to explain the dynamics and history that surround the situation. It is important to understand how my family got to where we are today and how putting my coaching skills to work has helped us move forward into a tomorrow filled with hope and possibilities.

We were a very happy family of four: my husband, Bruce, and me, and our two young daughters, Natalie and Olivia. The life we built together seemed perfect. Bruce and I had a loving relationship and two beautiful daughters—we were a foursome who loved to spend time together, travel together and seek adventure. We truly enjoyed being together, but as the girls got older, we all yearned for more. What began as a simple discussion about adopting a boy from a foreign country quickly escalated into an all-encompassing plan to grow our family.

Eight months later, we were all on a plane to Guatemala to meet our new addition. He was five months old and beautiful. We loved and needed him as much as he needed us. We spent an unforgettable week with him, traveling through Guatemala, learning about his magical country, learning about him and growing our family. Blessed! We felt very blessed!!

Late one night, on Olivia's seventh birthday, in the middle of this mysterious country, something horrible happened; something that would change our lives forever: Olivia had a seizure.

As I held her in the shower, her shaking seemed endless. She was a rag doll in my arms, shaking uncontrollably. At that time, I thought she was having trouble breathing due to a croupy cough from which she had been suffering. I mistakenly thought she was struggling to breathe and that that was causing the unusual shaking. I had no idea this was a seizure. I kept thinking, *I can't believe this is happening in the middle of the night, in the middle of nowhere, so far from modern civilization. Just breathe Olivia, just breathe!*

Her shaking went on for so long that I thought it might never end. But by the time my husband had returned from frantically searching for a doctor, she was just about done with this episode. Finally, the trembling subsided, and she fell asleep in his arms. I let out a long breath. *It's over, it's over, she's going to be okay.* "Over" was exactly what this wasn't; it was actually just the *beginning*, the beginning of a long, horrible road. A road filled with detours, bumps, hills, sharp curves and battlefields. It is a road I never expected to be on, let alone be driving on.

After that first seizure in Guatemala, Olivia had seizures nearly every day for over a year—sometimes over twenty times a day. She was no longer able to attend school, interact with family or friends, and basically never left the house. Her only outing was to the hospital where she was nearly a full-time resident. She blew through twelve different medications in eleven months, with no relief. She was a mere shadow of the sweet, carefree child she had once been. Eventually, she would endure five brain surgeries, hundreds of blood draws, scans, spinal taps and months of therapy—all with a smile on her face and laughter in her heart. And always, always, clinging to hope!

A clear diagnosis proved difficult to get. Pathology was confusing and sometimes misleading. During the years of numerous MRIs, surgeries, and EEG monitoring, we were given hope, and then it was torn away. More light was seen, only to be followed by darkness. The roller-coaster ride of extreme ups and downs played with our minds, tore our hearts apart and drove us nearly insane. Through this time, a very ominous, black cloud hung over our heads. Things were unclear. All of the pieces of the puzzle hadn't come together. Periodically, Olivia did well, giving us hope. In August 2008, she finally returned to our local elementary school and we all celebrated.

At some point during our journey, I became a support system for many families of the neurology and neurosurgery departments at the hospital. Families found their way to me so I could share our story, learn about theirs and help them find hope and courage. As I began spending more time helping these distraught families, I discovered that empowering people to believe in themselves was a true calling; it's how I wanted to spend my life. I quickly found an amazing coaching school, and my life with coaching began.

After I experienced my first series of training sessions and started my course work, I felt an overwhelming passion for what I was learning. I was energized to soak in all the material, to practice my growing skills and to strategically plan how I would run my business. My head was spinning as I plotted my new business life and direction. After three-and-a-half long, difficult years, I was finally able to give something back to myself. I wasn't just "Olivia's mom," I was *Stephanie* again, and I was on my way to becoming a professional life coach.

Then, it happened again: two weeks after returning from my second series of training sessions, Olivia had a seizure. A big one; a kind she had never had before. A seizure unlike the others. She hadn't had any problems for months. *How is this possible? She'd been doing so well!* We had all thought she was on the road to recovery and had let our guards down. We believed we were moving past this. Damn!

The best way to teach love is to *be* love

Soon, Olivia was having daily seizures and wasn't able to attend school. After a few weeks, she insisted on going back to class even if she was seizing. She was "comfortable" having seizures again and felt able to work through them at school if given the chance. To make her transition back to the class as easy as possible, I went in and gave a mini-seminar on epilepsy and shared a bit about Olivia's story. The children were very curious, asked a lot questions and seemed eager to see her again. By the end of the week, I found a folder in Olivia's backpack filled with letters from the students. They wrote beautiful words reassuring Olivia that they would help her fight to find a cure for epilepsy and that they were her friends—no matter what; strong words straight from the heart.

Life offers neither problems nor challenges, only opportunities.

That folder of letters sparked an idea that has since mushroomed into an enormous undertaking for our family. I asked Olivia how she would have felt to read those types of letters when she first began having seizures. Her eyes lit up and an idea was born. Our family could write a book about epilepsy and how it *affects* your life, but how it doesn't have to *dictate* your life. Most of it would be from Olivia, but Natalie would write a chapter on siblings' feelings, and Bruce and I would address the parents. We have been meeting once a week about the book. I interview the girls and ask them direct, empowering questions, coaching them all the way to find their deepest answers. The insight I have gained has proven to be invaluable. Our book sessions provide raw, emotional insight into the hearts of our daughters. Not only are we building an amazing book to help others, but I am learning how to lead and help two little girls who desperately need direction and inspiration through a very confusing time.

After a new series of MRI scans and tests, the final report came in. The dark cloud that had been hovering above us for so long was now focused directly on Olivia, bearing down. Sadly, we were told the grim diagnosis. The disease was the one that robs your child of her mind, then physical capabilities; the one that destroys half of your child's brain, eventually killing the child; that was: Rasmussen's encephalitis. Very rare, very heartbreaking. *Is there any treatment? Is there any cure?* Yes, there is—as rare and as radical as the disease itself: a hemispherectomy to stop the destruction, essentially removing one-half of the child's brain—*one half!* In 2009, that's the best we've got—it is unthinkable.

Remarkably, after a hemispherectomy, the other side of a

child's brain will pick up most cognitive functions, memories, and personality, but will leave a tremendous physical deficit on the opposite side of the body. In Olivia's case, she will wake up talking, understanding, and cognitively functioning without constant debilitating seizures, but in exchange, she will have to give up physical movement of her entire left side. She will wake up partially paralyzed; essentially a 10-year-old baby, physically. Eventually, she will learn to hold her head up, sit and stand on her own, but forever have a significant weakness on her left side, as well as loss of the use of her hand, limited vision, and walk with a limp.

The greatest freedom is the freedom of choice. —Victor Frankel

As a mother, this is not what you expect. It is never what you plan for. It is sickening to consider and mentally process. It is maddening, frightening, deeply troubling, and very sorrowful. But it is all we have. It is hope. It is a future. I remind myself we have been given a choice that can save Olivia. *We have a choice!* Not a great choice, but a choice. We were given a way to save our child, and I know many parents who would give anything to be in our place. We know many children who would choose our journey instead of theirs, if given the chance.

I have been faced with many dilemmas. *How do I continue to lead this beautiful, courageous child through the darkest time of her life? How do I help our other children move past the hurt, the pain, the anger and the confusion? What can I do to find peace within myself to carry my battered crew? How can I help those around us view this as an opportunity for a better life? And how can I keep convincing myself?* I decide to read my Coaching Foundation Principles every day for ten minutes before I attack the day. I read and ponder them slowly, relating each to our current challenge, and finding hope within the meaning behind the words. This helps. It helps a lot!

I have also begun coaching myself on what I can do to find peace, inner strength and outer energy. I know I will need all of these going into surgery, but I am able to recognize that I need them now, as well. I reflect and talk with my own coach and with my husband about how we have gotten through the last three years; how we have survived; how our marriage has thrived in the midst of a tsunami crashing down on our life. I begin to connect the dots and analyze it all. I come with up with *faith*. Defying all logic and reasoning, I have felt that, no matter what challenges came her way, Olivia would overcome them. I always had faith in her. Faith in our family. Faith in our marriage. Faith in myself. And I have found that *faith is more powerful than truth*.

One of the greatest parts of my coach training has been that you get a lot of practice, and you *need* a lot of practice; so that's good. Coaching is tough in the beginning, because, naturally,

> *"None of their lives is about us—*
> *it's all about them!"*

most of us just want to fix things for others by giving advice on what we think they should do. However, as time passes, we realize this isn't about us, or about what we know, or who we know. It's about our clients. It's about their needs, their perspectives and their perceptions. None of their lives is about us—it's all about them! This is a difficult and enlightening concept to master, but when it is accomplished, it shapes our entire approach and interaction with others. Once I truly recognized this and started living it, I began seeing the changes within our family. Natalie, usually emotionally cut off from all uncomfortable feelings, began sharing real worries and concerns over Olivia's path. Olivia shared insight that confirmed to me she was ready, willing and able to attack the new detour she had been given. This is a gift many parents aren't ever able to share with their children. I feel blessed!

Pain is inevitable, suffering is optional —Buddhist proverb

When I began talking with Olivia about Rasmussen's and the surgery, she obviously had a lot questions and concerns. One of the first was, "Will I be able to play soccer afterward"? I reassured her that she would and heard myself saying, "But perhaps in a different league than before. Maybe a league for other kids who have faced some physical challenges might be a more competitive arena for you." She retorted, "So if there isn't one, maybe you and Daddy and Natalie and I could start a league for kids with disabilities—that way we'd know I would make the team, because we'd be in charge of it!" That is Olivia! That is why I know she will overcome the immense physical hurdles that will initially be put on her plate, and that is why she will do it with a smile, with a whole lot of humor, and definitely some sassy talk!

Why? Why has my sweet, caring, selfless daughter been faced with such a horrific illness? Why has our family suffered in every conceivable way because of this disease and its insidious progression? Why should any child have to endure invasive surgeries, painful recoveries, and grueling rehabilitation? Why do the other children in the family have to fight for attention and time because their parents are often too worn out to give them what they deserve?

I could write a novel on the pain and suffering that we have endured. I could fill a decade of appointments in a therapist's chair to relive the horror and the misery. *But why? Why would I want to? What benefit does it bring me, my children, or my husband to wallow in the anger and the sadness?* I am at a point in my journey that points to a different plan. A plan that tells me that we are each here for a special purpose.

I know, in my heart, that I am here to be a leader, a real coach. First, to coach our family, then others. I know that Natalie's quiet reserve in her sister's illness and recovery will set a path that will lead her as she grows. I am confident that our son, Ever, will continue to connect to the depth of love within our family and that he will forever remain Olivia's best buddy and cohort in crime. I believe, with all my heart, that if a child had to be created to smile, laugh, and say, "Bring it on," to any challenge, that child is Olivia. She will find her special purpose—and others will benefit from her experience. Her losses and her pain will not be in vain.

A purpose can be found in everything that happens.

Olivia is insightful. She can see the overwhelming amount of tasks I have taken on. My husband is on a tight work schedule, traveling frequently, trying desperately to make a dent in the mounting medical bills. I am working, studying, coaching, being a mom to Natalie and Ever, and I have her by my side most of the day and night. On a slow day, it is a fire drill. One morning, I found a bookmark on my calendar that Olivia had gotten from epilepsy camp. One side was printed, "IMAGINE! You Can Do It!" The other side had been left blank and she wrote, "Mommy you will make a perfect life coach! Love, Olivia."

I know I wouldn't have found coaching if it weren't for Olivia's illness and my involvement with many families through the hospital. She knows that, too. She also knows she wouldn't have met one of her very best friends if both families hadn't been affected by seizures. She casually mentions that we never would have had the chance to live in Miami and make friends there, if it weren't for her seizures. She loves raising money for the Epilepsy Foundation and enjoys competing with her nurses and doctors to out-raise them. She gets it!

It is difficult preparing for this unthinkable surgery. It is discouraging to envision the journey ahead. Facing moments of doubt, conflict, and anger became part of my daily battle as we inched closer to surgery. Energy attracts like energy. I regroup. I kick myself in the butt and remember that, if I focus on the negative and self-pity, that is exactly what I'll get. If I focus on hope and faith, I will receive hope and faith. I know I will get there.

I know I will become an incredibly busy, tremendously effective, professional life coach—outside of my family. But first, I am leading "Team Olivia" and the most amazing recovery anyone has ever seen. Most parents get to see their children sit up, stand and walk during one short phase of life. I have been given the pleasure of seeing it twice. Most children learn to stand, to walk, to run when they are too young to understand or appreciate it. Olivia will know the magnitude of these events. She will celebrate and feel each accomplishment. She will know she has achieved an amazing feat, and that will be a beautiful thing.

Every day now is heaped with positive thinking on what we desire, believe and can accept. My education to become a life coach has dramatically changed my life and helped me cope with an unthinkable situation. It is helping me lead my family and show them happiness where many thought it couldn't be found. And that is priceless!

I never saw it coming. I don't know where this road will go and how many potholes we'll need to swerve around to keep on the right path, but I know now that I'm a good driver. I believe in myself and adore my cargo. My heart and mind tell me that my Navigator will have my back; He always does. He will drive when I am weary. Together, we will steer the best we can and find peace and joy along the way. I have faith that my crew will arrive happy, healthy and ready to take on the world.

As I close my journal, I realize how far we've come, the unexpected ways we've grown, and the perspective that we've gained. My eyes go back to Olivia. She's lying completely still, almost frozen. Her bandaged head looks too heavy for her narrow neck to support. She looks vulnerable, weak and fragile. I remind myself this isn't the end. It's the beginning. For us, it's the beginning of recovery.

Each part of our journey out of PICU has been different, and something tells me that each one of these innocent children will leave here to move on to their next phase, whatever that might be. As I lay my head on the foot of Olivia's bed, I send positive healing energy to their families and their leaders. Being a leader is tough, I know. Sometimes, the task seems overwhelming, too much to even mentally process. Numerous times, I've met with parents who felt completely depleted from life's daily challenges and fear they are not effective leaders for their children. What I have found is that those with the least hope are the ones in which the most hope can be found. And hope is what life is about: hope for strength, hope for potential, hope for peace, hope for joy and hope throughout the journey. Hope is why I became a professional life coach; it's why I am able to live my life's purpose and passion, while helping others discover theirs.

There's a Coach in My Mirror!

JOURNEY 8

TIM DURLING

A life coach. I am a life coach! That's who I am. That's who I've been for longer than I realized. It is in me, a part of me, a part that's been waiting to be recognized, awakened and developed. One day, there was indeed a spark of acknowledgment.

I am a fan of inspirational speakers like Wayne Dyer and Marianne Williamson. They came to my home town of Tampa, Florida, in October 2008, as part of Louise Hay's "I Can Do It" conference. I signed up. Wayne was the kickoff keynote speaker on a Friday evening, and I was blown away by one of my heroes. I had watched him on his PBS specials for years and owned several of his books. A very nice evening indeed.

I returned to the Tampa Convention Center the next morning to choose from a list of simultaneous workshops and sessions with various authors and speakers. I had intended to leave early that day to get home in time for church. Church was important to me, and I reasoned that I would miss less of the conference by catching the late Saturday church service than by attending any of the Sunday services. But I was so engrossed in the speakers, as well as the energy of the people attending the conference, that there was no leaving for me. I was into this conference!

I met many fine and interesting people from all over the country. Early in the day, I was chatting with a nice woman from Maryland, who sat next to me while we waited for one of the speakers to begin. I was in tune with the high energy in the room; I was happy to be where I was, and I was anxious to talk and share. A few minutes into the conversation, she asked, "Tim, are you a life coach?" I hesitated and responded, "What's a life coach?" I will never forget that moment. It was the beginning of a new beginning.

She shared with me that she was a life coach and gave me a description of what she and other life coaches do. I was very interested. She exclaimed, "Tim, you need to be a life coach!" "You think so?" I replied. "Tim, you are a natural life coach. You have the passion and the energy," she shared. I thanked her, and the session speaker was ready to begin. I enjoyed the speaker, but I

> " *'Tim, you are a natural life coach.*
> *You have the passion and the energy.'* "

must admit that, occasionally, my mind jumped back to what my new friend had just shared. It felt good. It felt exciting. Something felt right. Something felt like she had touched a nerve, a volcanic nerve. I had a tinge of intrigue.

By the end of that day, many other people had asked me if I was a life coach. *What is this? Why do they think I am a life coach? I am a business guy with a business degree. I have spent a whole career in corporate America programming, upgrading software, analyzing business solutions, managing projects and help desks and IT departments. Why do these people think this company man is a life coach?* But the energy of this conference and the people there made me feel good, inspired, and lighter than usual. I know I smiled a lot, and I remember I ended up being one of the last people to leave the convention center that evening. I remember that I didn't want to miss anything.

The next morning, I was up bright and early to head back to the conference. I recall feeling very happy as I arrived. Excited to start the day, I jumped on the escalator to get to the second floor and chatted with those around me. Strangers? Yes, but kindred spirits I felt connected to, as well. Someone near me said, "You're very happy this morning." I said, "Yes. I had a great day yesterday. I think I went to sleep with a smile on my face last night, and I woke up with it still there this morning!" People laughed. I was not my old, stuffy, corporate self. Something had touched me and, although I didn't really understand it then, I knew I felt really good and that I was going to have another great day, and that I did.

Besides all the great authors and speakers at the conference, I met some incredible people in the vendor area. I bought several unique and meaningful items, but one booth, called "Reflect" (www.reflectmylife.com), stands out in particular. I met a brother-and-sister team there who were giving up their careers as chemical engineers to promote entrepreneurial dreams with a brainchild T-shirt company. They sell Ts with inspirational messages on the chest, in backward lettering, so that the message is forward and readable every time you pass in front of a mirror. *What a great idea—and which of the inspirational messages best defines the intense energy I feel in this moment?* I scanned the racks and the catalogs with my new friends, Drew and Caroline, and, although I wouldn't accept the obvious choice without making sure I had looked at every single option, the T for me was indeed obvious. White letters written backwards on black material, my message, my new mantra, my purpose in life was summed up then and there: "I change lives!" At that moment, I knew my life was changed. I knew that the lives of others would be changed through me, as well.

Better Bonding, Better Careers

ANTHONY FASANO

My life before coaching

When I was younger, my father always told me, "You can do anything you put your mind to." Well, I believed him, and I have lived, and continue to live, by that saying throughout my life. It has helped me to always have the confidence to strive for and achieve my personal and professional goals.

My parents were always 100 percent supportive of my brothers and me through all aspects of our lives and, for that, I am grateful. I grew up with two brothers; we always had a lot of fun together and still do, to this day. I always knew they would do great things and they have—I just never knew what I was going to do. Growing up, I always loved motivational speakers, books and inspirational quotes. I can always hear Tony Robbins telling me to take "massive action" in my life. These types of books and videos always hit home with me, for some reason, but I never knew why.

In high school, I really enjoyed my math and science courses, so in looking at colleges, I found engineering to be a good match for me. I received both undergraduate and graduate degrees in civil engineering. I chose the field because I liked the idea of having the opportunity to work outdoors at times and, of course, civil engineers have a huge impact on our society, being responsible for designing our bridges, buildings, roadways, and water- and waste-water systems.

College was a lot of fun. Why wouldn't it be? After all, it is college! I made a decision, early on in my college years, that I was

65

going to experience as many opportunities as I could over those four years and really get the most out of them. Well, I surely did just that. First and foremost, I met my wife during freshman year, in Engineering 101. We built a magnetically levitated train and a concrete canoe (yes, concrete) with fellow civil engineering students, which was then entered into a contest. I volunteered to organize a civil-engineering job fair, which brought engineering companies to the school to assist seniors in obtaining postgraduate employment. I participated in several intramural sports, like flag football and floor hockey, which were fun experiences. I worked in the computer lab, assisting students with computer questions and challenges.

Other than meeting my wife, about whom I will write more later, there were two other life-changing experiences that I took from my college years. One of them was joining a fraternity. I became a brother of Kappa Delta Rho in my sophomore year of college. For those of you who don't know, in order to join a fraternity, you and your fellow "pledges" must go through a pledging

"It blew me away that a group of seventeen people could function as one."

period where the brothers pretty much make you do anything and everything as a "test" or "admissions process" into the fraternity. The experience was amazing for many reasons, but the one reason that stuck out for me was the connection that was created between all of us pledges. It was like we were instantly one person.

It blew me away that a group of seventeen people could function as one. It didn't matter whether you liked or disliked one of your pledge brothers, we were simply a pledge class with a common goal, and we stuck together to do whatever we had to do to get there. We were put through some extremely difficult and uncomfortable situations, and some pledges quit, but those of us who stuck together and made it through, still have a brotherly relationship to this day. It was the first time in my life that I felt that type of unity with a group like that. I had played sports growing up and was always close with my teammates, but had never felt a bond like that.

The semester after we pledged, I was presented with the opportunity to study abroad, in Brussels, Belgium. This was a difficult decision, because I had just gone through the experience with my fraternity brothers described above, and I was now faced with the decision of leaving all these new brothers for six months. I thought very long and hard about it, and I discussed it with my wife (my girlfriend, at the time), who was also considering going abroad. We decided to do it, and those six months abroad were the most amazing of my life.

Studying overseas opened up my mind to a whole other world! For the first time in my life, I realized that there were actually other countries and people in this world. Being raised in America, I was very narrow-minded and knew only the culture that I was surrounded with. In Europe, every two-hour car ride presented me with a whole new nationality, government, language, currency and general outlook on life.

To make it even more interesting, Brussels, the city in which we lived, was split right down the middle. Half of the city was of a Dutch background and spoke Flemish, and the other half of the country was French-speaking. My wife was on the Dutch side of the city, and I was on the French side. So, just by visiting her host family across town, the entire experience changed.

While we were there, we visited thirteen countries all over Europe, whose cities included London, Paris, Madrid, Barcelona, Rome, Florence, Milan, Vienna, Amsterdam and more. Never did I think I would get to see all of those cities in a lifetime, and especially not at the age of nineteen. The memories, including the five photo albums that we have from that trip, will last forever, and all because we made a decision to take the trip, which, at the time, was a very difficult decision to make. Looking back now, it should have been a no-brainer to take off a semester of college and visit thirteen European countries. Many decisions are easier when you look back on them, but, at the time, giving up a semester of college was tough to do. It was this experience abroad that truly started opening up my mind to see all of the opportunities in the world.

When I graduated, I took a job with a civil-engineering company, and everything came naturally to me in the way of career development. The drive and motivation that I had to advance my career were exciting. I just wanted to keep flying higher and higher. I noticed that, through my years in engineering, I enjoyed most the relationships that I had built and the opportunities to meet as many people as I could along the way.

As my career progressed, I continued to advance so much that one day, my boss approached me and asked me to put together a seminar on career development to present to the other engineers in the company. The results of the seminar were powerful, and the engineers I spoke to started taking huge steps in their career because of the seminar. Not only was I able to help make a difference in their careers, but I absolutely loved doing it!

After one of the seminars, I went home, and I remember sitting on the couch telling my wife, "Jill, I think I can do this on a regular basis as my job." My wife asked, "Do what?" I said, "Inspire people and help them move their careers and their lives forward." I had told her that I heard something about coaching and that I was going to look into it. Even though I didn't know much about coaching, something about the idea of it felt right to me. My wife, whom I had met in college, as I pointed out earlier, has always stood by me in all of my crazy endeavors, from a multilevel marketing business to investing in four rental properties. She has always supported me, and I am grateful to her for that. During that period, we were going through a very stressful time having a young child and a tough pregnancy, which was putting extra strain on us. So, there on the couch that night, with a three-year-old daughter and my wife pregnant with our second, she told me that if coaching was what I wanted to do, she would support me. That was all I needed to hear!

I immediately started searching for a coaching school, and my search led me to the Institute for Professional Excellence in Coaching (iPEC). I enrolled in the New York City class, but noticed that I had just missed the first weekend of training for the current New York schedule. Therefore, I was faced with a difficult decision: I could either wait for six months to start my iPEC journey, or I could pack my bags and drive four hours to Massachusetts, that upcoming weekend, to take the class up there. With my wife's support and my dream of doing what I have always wanted to do, I packed my bags and never looked back.

During that car ride to Massachusetts, I experienced some of the most liberating hours of my life. Cruising up the highway, I knew this was one of the best decisions I had ever made, and the coming months would surely confirm those feelings.

The iPEC experience transformed both my personal and professional lives. It is very difficult to put into words how powerful the iPEC experience was for me, but I will start by writing about my fellow coaching students. If you recall, I wrote earlier about the bond that was created among my fellow fraternity brothers and me. Well, the bond I felt with my fellow iPEC coaching students was one hundred times stronger.

Through many interactive components of the training, we students got to know one another on both a personal and professional level. Spending a weekend with twenty or thirty motivated, determined, inspired, high-energy people is an amazing experience. Through the iPEC program, I was able to experience that four different times. Having the opportunity to connect with people on a similar, yet different, journey was very rewarding.

In addition to giving me the skills needed to become a great coach, the iPEC training provided me with nine months of phenomenal personal growth and development. It helped me to not only discover my purpose in life, but to shift my outlook on life to see the opportunity in everything that happens. This outlook alone has helped me to inspire professionals and businesses, as well as my family, my friends, my neighbors, and myself, in a powerful way.

My coaching experience so far

My first paying client hired me one month into my coaching training, and that gave me the confidence to immediately start building my coaching business. I put a lot of thought into my company name and decided on Powerful Purpose Associates, because I believe that there is a powerful purpose in what we, as coaches, do.

Early in my coaching business, I decided to start sending out a

Monday morning motivational email to help people start off their week in a positive way. I called it the *Monday Morning Motivator* (*MMM*), and it focuses on a quote or thought of the week and includes a message from me as to how the thought applies to our careers, businesses and lives. My list of recipients started with about thirty people locally, and it is already up to two hundred people worldwide, and it is growing rapidly. I have received a very positive response from these messages.

Just recently, I ran into a friend of a friend at the bank, and he thanked me for the motivational messages that are keeping him going. My goal is to send this *MMM* to as many people as possible, because I believe that the more people I can help to start off the week positively, the more positive energy and attitudes will spread through our families, our communities and the world. Please visit our website at www.powerfulpurpose.com to sign up for our *Monday Morning Motivator,* or email me directly at afasano@powerfulpurpose.com.

We have also created a blog dedicated to career development and advancement, and we send out a daily email called *A Daily Boost from Your Professional Partner,* to inspire professionals every day.

Even during my coaching training, my business did very well for being so young. I worked with seven clients and really enjoyed it. I knew that I had found my calling. I was also able to help many of my coaching peers start their businesses, as I have a natural passion for career and business growth and development.

Thanks to one of the books we read for our training, *Book Yourself Solid,* by Michael Port, I created a career-development program called the Career-Biz Booster Program. Please check out www.careerbizboost.com. The program is based on the six points that I believe are critical to our growth and development of a career and/or business. The program provides professionals and business owners with a professional coach to help them develop these six points, in an effort to succeed beyond their expectations. I have started giving seminars on the program to engineers, and the feedback has been extremely positive.

Where I see myself going with my coaching business

Through my coaching business, Powerful Purpose Associates, I intend on helping thousands of professionals and businesses grow and develop to be as successful as they choose to be. My main goal is to bring coaching into the engineering world and other industries, to inspire as many people as I can to move their businesses and careers forward in a way that is enjoyable and rewarding to both them and their companies.

I intend on utilizing a combination of my Career-Biz Booster Program and the iPEC Energy Leadership Development System to help companies transform by inspiring their professionals to enjoy their highest potential. This creates a win/win scenario as the professionals realize a more enjoyable, less stressful career, and the companies enjoy higher levels of success in employee morale and satisfaction, company growth, and increased profits.

I intend to speak in front of thousands of people to let them know they have the absolute choice to take their personal and professional lives wherever they want to take them. As my father always told me, "You can do anything you put your mind to." Through my *Monday Morning Motivator*, public speaking and coaching, I plan on spreading that message to as many people as I can!

Grace and Life Purpose

TINA FRIZZELL-JENKINS

According to a bestselling book, "God is able to make all grace abound to you, so that in all things at all times, having all that you need, you may abound in every good work." (*2 Corinthians*, 9:8) *Webster* defines the word *abound* as, to be plentiful, to exist in large numbers, to be filled, having abundance, and being wealthy. Therefore, if we insert the definition into the scripture, it would read something like this:

> "God is able to make grace plentiful to you, so that, in all things, at all times, having all that you need, you may be plentiful or wealthy, in every good work."

Wow! I believe every life has a purpose. Couple life's purpose with grace and awesome things are possible—and they occur. My life/journey speaks to that.

I am a Washingtonian. I was born and raised in our great nation's capital Washington, DC. My loving and highly supportive parents are Tillman and Aretha Frizzell. They still live in the house they built for us in the city. I was born the middle child, between two delightful brothers that I affectionately call Tony and Li'l Till (5'11½"), and who contributed to making life, growing up, interesting and fun. My paternal grandparents lived in the house next door, and I had a host of other relatives who lived nearby.

On many memorable occasions, several of those relatives, if not all, would convene on the porch and in the yard of my grandparents. A lot of laughter and family discussions took place there.

I like to believe that my grandfather's quiet, loving and gentle nature contributed to my demeanor, while my grandmother's creativity and faith registered on my radar at an early age.

I was educated in the public school system, in which the great majority of my teachers were nurturing, caring and all-around great educators. In elementary school, it became obvious that learning would be a challenge for me. It was in third grade that two teachers pulled me aside and quizzed me on some basic math. They asked, "What is seven plus seven?" I would quickly reply, "fourteen." Then they would ask, "What is seven plus eight?" I would hesitate, think and calculate to get the answer of fifteen. They would quiz me on several similar problems and get the same responses.

It was clear to them that I should have been able to respond just as quickly to the second question as I did the first, because I had only to realize that I needed to add one to my previous answer to get the next answer. I remember seeing the puzzlement in their eyes and hearing the comment, "See, she does not get it." It was also around the same time that I remember working with a speech therapist to assist me in speaking correctly. Add to that the fact that reading and reading comprehension were thorns in the flesh of my educational existence.

In sixth grade, I was chosen to give the sixth-grade graduation Welcome Address, for which I received a standing ovation. I also remember getting several acknowledgments and awards.

That journey of my life was the first in confirming that *God is able to make all grace abound to me, so that, in all things, at all times, having all that I need, I may be plentiful.* Grace put the correct people in my life to assist me in my learning challenges. Grace gave me parents who inspired me. Grace brought out my ability to remember things, whether I understood them or not. Grace provided me with the platform of which I could give a speech and build my confidence.

It was in junior high school that I met my high-school sweetheart, the wonderful man to whom I have been married for the past twenty-five years; after dating all through high school and college. I worked hard in junior high to keep a B–B+ average, and that is also where my athletic abilities flourished. Track and field

and basketball were my sports of choice. I excelled in track because I was quick, and, though I was not much of a shooter in basketball, I was a great defensive player and could steal the ball. I
was good at sports, but I did not love them. Perhaps I had the
ability, but I did not have the passion to be great. Oddly enough,
I was more interested in getting academic awards than trophies
and medals.

By the time I graduated from junior high, I was sure I wanted
to conquer the monster of academic learning. It was grace that
gave me direction in that season of my life. It was grace that afforded me the gall to presume I could accentuate my intellect,
which did not appear to be my best quality.

It was in high school, H.D. Woodson, that I had the time of
my life. I was voted the friendliest in our senior yearbook. I developed friendships that I still cherish today. I was inducted into
the National Honor Society in my junior year. I graduated nine-
teenth in my class of over six hundred, and I was vice president of
my graduating class. Don't get me wrong; I had to study twice as
hard as everyone else to get the results I got.

It was in high school that I decided to pursue engineering in
college, after completing a summer program in engineering at
Howard University and working on and solving an engineering
traffic project in the city, through a program at the school. However, I had a high-school math teacher who told me I was not engineering material. She said that, although I was doing well in
math, it was too much of a struggle for me, and I would not make
it through engineering math. The comment stung, but I was familiar with the concept of *grace*.

I went on to college, where the road was rough and the obstacles plentiful. Fun was in limited quantities, and it was there that
I had an advisor who suggested I take another career path. My
struggles were not worth it, in his opinion. During this journey
of my life, my mom would regularly send me positive affirmations
from Success Motivation Institute, a franchise she had acquired,
to display around my room.

Therefore, I reached back into my memory and recalled that
*God is able to make all grace abound to me, so that, in all things, at all
times, having all that I need, I may abound in every good work.*

I finished my undergraduate work, earning a B.S. in mechanical engineering from Northeastern University, in December of 1983; and I walked with the Class of 1984. Northeastern, at the time, was the largest private institution with the best cooperative education program. By the time I graduated, I had a year-and-a-half of on-the-job experience, which afforded me the opportunity to obtain a job with a very nice, entry-level salary. I recall going to the bank to cash my paycheck and getting speculative glances, when the bank teller would see the amount, then look at my identification, and then back at me. For a twenty-three year old (who looked more like an eighteen year old), African-American female, that was a substantial paycheck at that time. Given that, you might imagine that bankers were a little skeptical.

I started my professional career in the private sector in January of 1984. I worked for a company called E-System—Melpar Division in Falls Church, Virginia. This was the same company for which I had worked as a co-op student, starting back in 1981. The company's production was military electronics. The following September, I was married to Willis at our family church, Ward Memorial AME, in the District of Columbia. My husband and I both enjoyed employment at E-Systems until May of 1989, when I started government employment with NASA's Goddard Space Flight Center in Greenbelt, Maryland, as a facilities engineer. In this position, it was my job to effectively manage the design and construction of state-of-the-art laboratories and facilities that supported the science and the missions.

In November of 1989, our first daughter, Tinille, was born, and, in 1992, we welcomed our second daughter, Tenise. In 1994, my husband joined me as a government employee at NASA, working on the mission as an electrical engineer. In 1995, I obtained a general contractor's permit, and my husband and I designed and built our second home. Imagine with me the excitement of being able to build my own home. This is something of which I had dreamed as a young child. I went through the county's permitting process and was approved. Our finances were in order. I put together "one of the best loan packages I have ever seen," according to our bank agent. She told me everything looked great, and she only had to go to the vice president to get a cursory signature. She said it would be no problem because everything was in order.

She called me back with hesitation and amazement in her voice. She said Mr. V.P. would not sign, and there were no reasons given. I talked to the vice president and, to make a long story short, he did not believe in me despite my qualifications. He offered to loan me as much money as I needed to purchase a house, but I was not interested in his offer. I felt I was being mistreated because I was a young, black female, and it hurt.

Around that time, Mom had to remind me of grace, and she advised me to contact my congressman. The very next day, after the vice president was contacted by the congressman's office, my construction loan was miraculously approved. The vice president called to let me know and to threaten me with, "I will not give you a cent more for overruns." Grace not only allowed us to start building, it allowed us to get our U & O (Use & Occupancy) in seven months, with a few thousand dollars left in the bank. In my life, this was one of the "all things" in which grace abounded.

Prior to starting a new professional career as a facilities engineer, I started on a private career path that would eventually lead me, twenty-plus years later, to the Institute for Professional Excellence in Coaching (iPEC). Along with my husband, I started a service company called Advance Auto Consultants, Inc. The company assisted mostly women in the purchase of a new car, without the haggling, and at a great price. The service was needed because it was a known fact, especially at the time, that women were being taken advantage of when purchasing a car.

It was at this point in our lives, that it became obvious we had to learn how to keep the money we were making and not let taxes consume the fruits of our labor. We also discovered that it was necessary to attach ourselves to mentors who could teach us what most people never thought to, or knew to learn. Later, we would start another service company, called Just Traders International (JTI), LLC. This became the umbrella company for transportation services and home-based-business tax-awareness services. Through these business experiences and attaching ourselves to the correct people, we were able to put some practices in place that became worth sharing so others could benefit. For additional information, go to my website at www.tinafrizzell.com.

I started giving a PowerPoint presentation in my basement that not only encouraged home-based business owners to keep the money they earned, but it taught them how. Business owners were learning what could make the difference in getting a return of $10 versus $10,000. We established a website at www.seminar fortaxsavings.com.

As you might imagine, the seminars grew to the point that they were being hosted in libraries, meeting rooms and hotels. Not only did the seminars grow, but people started requesting individual support. While providing support, it became clear that I could better serve my clients if I could offer an additional skill set that I recognized to be coaching. It wasn't enough, at this point, to increase awareness and give direction and advice; I became interested in having my clients buy into their own success and the process to get there. Working with a coach could do that for the client.

As life would have it, I was becoming more and more dissatisfied in my NASA position. I no longer felt I was making a significant contribution, and a call went out to become a NASA coach. As I read the bulletin, it was as if the Coach's Council was asking for me personally. It was a way to enhance my career at NASA, while incorporating another skill into an interest that I really enjoyed. However, I interviewed, and the panel rejected me. In summation, I was told that I lacked the similar background, knowledge and experience that a supervisor would gain in developing personnel.

I was crushed. The panel did not see in me what I saw in myself. I felt like I had failed myself and all of the people whom I was supposed to walk alongside of and assist in reaching their potential. Somehow, I had fallen off course and surely jeopardized fulfilling my purpose.

Then I remembered, *God is able to make all grace abound to me, so that, in all things, at all times, having all that I need, I may abound in every good work.* Good work, in this case, was coaching, and I believed that I could be and would be plentiful. I pursued coaching as self-improvement with the support of my management. I found coaching to be the most awesome and rewarding self-development I had ever done, counting all the numerous self-growth classes I had enjoyed over the years.

A little more than halfway through the program, it became absolutely evident to me that I would be a coach. My pursuit of coaching and the willingness to conquer the quest on my own, got the attention of NASA's Coaching Council, and I was invited to be a member with them. I accepted the invitation, and I am pleased to be collaborating with the team.

Within the coaching cohort, coaching is done using different styles, skills, and techniques. Planting seeds (inch by inch, life is a cinch), visioning, and celebrating are a few skills my mom successfully put into practice with me, while I was growing up. Also, I am particularly drawn to a coaching technique, called The Three-Step Coaching Process. This technique explores (1) what is working well; (2) why it is working well; and (3) what specifically made it work. The technique helps you to build on your previously discovered strengths, resources, and gifts to achieve a current goal. This is a technique that I have been practicing, from a very young age, not knowing it to be used in the coaching world.

Here's how the Three-Step Coaching Process works: As an issue or obstacle arises in your life that seems unmovable or unbeatable, you reflect back to a point in time where you had overcome an obstacle and you remember what it was like to get the victory. You remember what you saw, what you smelled, what you heard, what you felt, and, perhaps, you remember how good the

> *"Coaching is a good work. Coaching is a service, and serving feeds my soul."*

victory meal was that you enjoyed after the ordeal. You use those feelings of success to create the energy, physically and mentally, to walk on the current trail, to the other side—success. For me, that's when I relied on past triumphs from which the victories stemmed because of grace.

Why? Because, *God is able to make all grace abound to you, so that, in all things, at all times, having all that you need, you may abound in every good work.*

Coaching is a good work. Coaching is a service, and serving

feeds my soul. Coaching is a piece of the puzzle of my life that makes me who I am. Therefore, I applaud iPEC in creating a spectacular program that uniquely prepared me to be a professional friend. I am someone who provides ongoing client stimulation and encouragement for personal improvement, while facilitating guidance towards life's purposes and goals. I am an empowerment coach who specializes in home-based business taxes, leadership and relationship-building.

Who Will Fix the Fixer?

RONIT HAKIMI

Shortly after I was born in Tehran, Iran, everybody sighed. They were all happy to see me enter the world, happy and healthy. They were even more ecstatic to know that my mom was alive and well. Three years prior, when she almost passed away giving birth to my older brother, she was told that she could never have children again and that her life depended on it. Being on this earth and living this life is a miracle in the making for my family and me, and I am finally beginning to realize the reasons why.

My parents and the four of us led a joyous and fulfilled life, constantly laughing, and surrounded with loving friends and family. That life suddenly came to an end when I was about four, with the overthrow of the shah of Iran and the institution of Ayatollah Khomeini. The country was in chaos—schools and businesses were closed, electricity was shut off, and public transportation was disrupted. There were constant demonstrations and yelling in the streets—the life we knew would never be again. We were informed that the airports were on the verge of closing and, for our safety, we should quickly leave the country. My mom and the four of us bought tickets, packed two suitcases and got on a flight to Israel. My father, who was the closest person to me at the time, remained behind, attempting to liquidate some assets and wrap up our lives in Iran.

The move was very difficult for all of us: a language barrier, a completely new culture and a new life. My mother had the hardest time, being alone, away from my father and my grandparents, and caring for four young children who were all terrified of this huge and sudden change. It was during those moments that my mom began to feel helpless, alone and at the mercy of life. It was as if she lost a part of herself with the move; a part that she would never again find.

After about two years, my father finally joined us. He was not able to accomplish much in Iran as far as asset liquidation; it was just too chaotic and corrupt. Instead, he left almost all his assets to my maternal grandparents to handle. Like my mother, my father also experienced a period where he was down and constantly blaming others for his situation and misfortune; however, he quickly found his place in the working and social worlds, and bounced back.

I remember, during those few years of transition, thinking how responsible I was for my mom's happiness, and how I should concentrate on making her proud and fulfilled. I began to feel accountable for the well-being of everyone surrounding me. I became more conscious about how my attitudes and behavior affected all those around me and, possibly, even those not around me. For the purpose of obtaining success with my new commitment, I made a promise to myself to never allow any circumstances to limit my miraculous outlook on life. Each moment is precious and pure. There is an opportunity of reinvention every second of every day. I chose to adhere to this philosophy, and I constantly reached for success and excellence in everything I did. I excelled in school, in sports and in volunteering. I was a great sister, a great friend and an awesome *everything* to those around me. I wanted to do it for my mother. I wanted to do it for my father. I wanted to be and live every possibility. Though my intention was pure and noble, my focus was external. Everything I did was for others, thinking that it was up to me to be responsible and to bring about greatness.

At the age of fifteen, the Intifada (the Palestinian uprising) began in Israel. My father was working with the Palestinians in a wholesale capacity, extending large sums of money to them via merchandise. Those monies became extremely difficult to recover once the borders to the areas primarily occupied by Palestinians were closed. Contrary to what I wanted, my parents decided to send me to the U.S., to join my three older siblings, who were already working and studying there. My parents were to stay be-hind for a couple of months to retrieve some of their monies and liquidate their assets. A couple of months turned into three years.

Moving to the U.S., away from my parents and friends, was challenging, to say the least. At school, the teachers and adminis-trators mistook my language barrier for a learning difficulty. I was placed in classes that were being taught at a level much lower than the one to which I was accustomed. I did not know anyone in school, and I could not confidently communicate with anyone, either. With the help of an incredible guidance counselor, Lou Vetri, who really took the time to listen to me and understood my true language challenge, I was placed in the appropriate-level classes and began to learn English. Mr. Vetri believed in me and propelled me forward with such momentum that I never looked back.

I became very active in high school and joined Starlight, Make A Wish Foundation, the yearbook committee and the track team. I quickly bridged the language and cultural gaps and graduated with honors. In college, most of the professors and students could not even tell that I was born and raised in a different country. I fit right in and was then able to go back to my former normal, heal-thy ways and patterns. I participated and excelled in the many dif-ferent activities with which I was engaged. I was constantly focus-ing on the needs of other people and the community surrounding me; always on a quest to "help," "fix" and be of service. Now that my family was away from me, I found a wide array of new audi-ences.

After graduation, I got a job as an executive trainee for Bloo-mingdale's and quickly became an executive; first on the retail floor and, later, in the flagship store in New York City, as a train-ing executive. I was responsible for developing training classes and seminars and administering live trainings for all the branch stores. The only thing more powerful than being at service to others, is teaching hundreds of employees how to be at service to others!

While working in Bloomingdale's, I met my husband. We got married and had two beautiful children. Both our lovable girls were born with special needs, and we decided that I would remain home with them to provide them with the best possible care and attention. Those years were the most challenging years of my life. I constantly focused on the needs of the children and was actively engaged in either seeking or providing solutions to their challenges. My world became all about the girls and their limitations; it was as if I had no capacity for anything else. My focus was not on opportunity or what is right; rather, it was more on *Why did this happen to us* and, after a while, *poor us?*

For the first time in my life, I began to identify with the feelings my mother had held onto after we left Iran: feelings of separation and doubt. The magnificence, abundance, growth and divinity of my family, and the world as a whole, was no longer revealed to me in my thoughts, emotions and actions. Instead, I chose to dwell on lack and limitation. I was, however, for an extended period of time, completely unaware of who I was being, what I was thinking, and what I was doing. I was like a horse with blinders on—moving in the dark, without a vision.

Around the time my youngest daughter turned one year old, I had an awakening; Somehow, I became conscious of the choices I was making, and I was shocked. I felt as if I was living in a body that was not my own and in a mind that I did not even know. My world revealed itself as foreign, strange and unfamiliar. Even though, for the first time in my life, I was not moving from one country, state or area to the next, I somehow managed to create that illusion for myself, my family and all those around me. I began a journey of self-love, self-discovery and self-fulfillment. I practiced awareness of the present moment and gratitude for what *is*, through different modalities, such as meditation, yoga, affirmations, reading and participation in transformational classes.

Throughout my journey, I felt that there was a missing link; a bridge that would enable me to connect to the divinity and the power within others and myself, from a space of love, understanding and non-judgment. That bridge of light and possibility was presented to me in the form of coaching. Becoming a coach has unleashed my belief in the innate ability that each and every one of us has to create and enjoy the life we desire. It has demonstrated to me how we choose our lives, one breath at a time, through the way we think, act and behave. That constant desire to serve, for the purpose of "improving" and "fixing" others, has subsided dramatically and, with it, the tremendous burden I was constantly feeling.

I now see how much more effective and powerful it is to provide others with tools for self-discovery and growth, rather than taking on their challenges and constantly being engaged in the

"...we choose our lives one breath at a time, through the way we think, act and behave."

act of feeling sorry, fixing and doing. This single insight alone has freed my spirit and energy tremendously. I am now able to look internally for answers that are aligned and in sync with who I am and what I believe, rather than looking externally, and get someone else's answers.

I now look at my children (and not only my own—all children) as a one-of-a-kind, divine gift from God. Not just for the numerous obvious reasons, but also because they have inspired me to work with families who have young children and to create programs for elementary schools. I have developed programs that foster powerful communication, self-esteem, confidence and self-love among young children and the people in their lives. As coaches, we learn to ask powerful questions that invoke curiosity and discovery. I would like to present you with two questions: What if the "Lou Vetri" experience could happen every day? What if other women could gain access to their higher power and unlimited possibility at any moment, even when facing challenges and tough transitions?

Throughout my life, I have attempted to come up with a purpose or an intention for my life—one that would capture my essence and values to guide me through my journey. I had attempted this task many times and never been able to develop one with which I felt satisfied. With the guidance of iPEC, I was able to finally discover my life purpose, and I would like to conclude by sharing it with you. Setting an intention has always been a solid, first step in success and—who knows?—in a year, this statement might be completely different!

"I, Ronit Kayour Hakimi, hear, see, feel and know that my purpose in life is to fully accept myself and know that I am accepted. To be present with each moment and intuitively connect to self and the universe at large. To live a peaceful abundant life with ease. To achieve my fullest potential in life—physically, mentally, emotionally and spiritually. To empower others to live a life of happiness, purpose and fulfillment. To confidently, powerfully, and passionately spread light and love upon my being and the being of all others I encounter."

L'chaim—a Hebrew cheer "to life!"

Let the Madness Cease

Sue Koch

My life prior to coaching was everything I thought it was supposed to be; what I was groomed to imagine for myself as a child. I was very "successful." My career path in technology started promptly after college, and I continued to move quickly up the ladder to executive management, over the next fourteen years. My friends and family looked up to me and were proud of me. Great job, salary, car, condo and lifestyle! That was who I was; what defined me, and I worked myself sick making sure that I didn't let go of that presumption of self.

If I was so "successful," why was I so miserable? Somewhere along the line, I accepted that this kind of success came with twelve- to fourteen-hour days, frustrations, and stress-induced health problems, while sacrificing family, an athletic past, and myself in getting the job done and rising to the next level. *One day, I'd enjoy the fruits of my labor! One day, I'd have enough money saved up to retire a little early and enjoy life, finally meet that "right" man, have some peace, and travel the world!*

My first message hit me like a truck: a phone call telling me my father had collapsed and was in the hospital. I was in Chicago; he was in the middle of nowhere, in a small town in Colorado. I scrambled to make sure I could see him. Something deep inside told me it would be my last chance. I didn't get that last chance. On the way to the airport, my mother called; he was already gone. I usually spoke with my parents weekly, but I'd missed my last phone call to Colorado. I was busy and had a meeting that night, but I told myself, "I'll see him soon." I had a visit planned to see them in two weeks and we'd catch up then. I still returned to Colorado, to spend that planned visit with my mother, who would be alone on what would have been their fifty-third wedding anniversary.

When I returned home, I went back to my routine with a vengeance, out of denial. In avoidance mode, I did what I did best: I worked nonstop—sometimes up to eighteen hours a day. What was likely an attempt to avoid the depression of grieving my father, came around and found me in the way of severe anxiety attacks and depression from stress and exhaustion. My body and my mind suffered.

I had a kick in the ass one day as I sat on my couch, pondering the fact that I just didn't care about anything anymore. It may sound crazy to some, but I literally did feel like something came through the couch and pushed me. I was sure it was my father giving me a shove. I found myself standing, putting on my running clothes and heading to the gym, without even thinking. It felt good! I was reminded of how I really processed well when running; my mind cleared and I was able to problem-solve. I decided I needed some kind of life change—I didn't know what yet—but something big. I had always felt a huge gap in my life, but couldn't pinpoint it. I had let it go unaddressed for so long, always thinking, "I'll figure it out one day." Therapy was fine for the grief, depression and anxiety, but for this, I needed a life coach.

I started to explore these feelings, my gremlins, what I was missing, what I was passionate about, what my values were, and how they aligned with how I was living my life. Something I found along the way was that, while I was working myself to the bone for any company, the thing I really cared about most was the people. I fnally discovered an alignment here: the coaching I was experiencing was also the coaching I wanted to provide.

That was when I decided to seek out training, and I found iPEC. I started down the path of coach training, and it initially proved to be exceptional for me in the way of personal awareness and growth. I was still being held back internally, however. My fears of supporting myself and maintaining a certain lifestyle were now joined by the fact that I was also helping to support a widowed, ill mother. This fueled that fire inside of me that told me I had to do anything I could to work hard to keep my job, make the company successful, and ensure the ongoing financial comfort for my family. I wanted to be sure my mother could be well taken care of. While I did not yet pursue coaching, what I didn't realize, at the time, was that the evolution was in progress.

During this period, I was the senior vice president of operations for a technology company. I deeply disagreed with how the business was run. The top values were fear and distrust, making it very difficult to accomplish anything of longevity or maintain a motivated employee base. This was in complete discord with my core values. It literally made me physically ill to operate in this way, but I felt I had to push through. I just didn't have time to find a new job while working twelve-hour days and taking care of an elderly parent. What I began to realize, yet again, was that my only moments of joy were when connecting with employees: helping people process ideas, mentoring, getting past complexities and conflict, and going to bat for people on a daily basis. Perhaps that dark cloud of distrust hanging over the office was the very thing that allowed me to hone in on the skills I'd felt I wasn't putting to use after my coach training. At some point, I realized that, just because I hadn't started a coaching practice (yet!), that didn't mean I wasn't being a coach.

And then, it happened again. My mom had been having many surgeries, and this last one was supposed to be the easiest—the one that was going to return my mother, finally, to some sense of normalcy and comfort, at least, for a while. Many complexities ensued, and my sister and I were suddenly faced with every child's most feared decision. We spent the next days watching her, talking to her and holding her hand, as our dear mother finally moved on to be with our father, once again.

This time, I became exceptionally angry at the world. My first reaction was to blame this horrible job I had, at which I worked so hard, for taking time away from my mother and other family members with whom I could have fostered relationships, but in my newfound self-awareness, I knew I had to take responsibility. In this moment, I decided to go back to iPEC. They welcomed me back as a student with open, supportive arms.

This time I was ready; ready for the change, ready to get outside of my comfort zone and explore the person I was supposed to be. I was ready to grieve, move forward and find that passion I'd been missing for so many years.

My evolution of self continued. I thought back to what I learned about my mother in the time I had spent with her. She brought so much pain from childhood into adulthood: fears and worries of not being good enough or worthy, all brought on by the hand and words of her father. It made me so sad that a woman seventy-eight years old had carried such beliefs with her for so long. I wondered what kind of improved health and happiness she might have been able to experience had such self-growth opportunities been available to her—or looked at more positively by her generation. This could have been me, too. I could have held onto fears of not being good enough; the belief that "this is what success is," while continuing to self-sacrifice, down a career path that made me ill and conflicted with my core being. I had to bring this awareness to others who did not yet have it, and to those who were already ready to explore it. What freedom!

As I discovered, I had to make drastic change. I started planning my next step. I realized that for five months already, I had been keeping a list of pros and cons for leaving my job. I came up with an extremely anal plan of which my father would have been very proud, walked into my CEO's office, and gave five weeks' notice. I came home and jumped up and down like a child. I knew that I had made the right decision!

What I dealt with next was expected, yet the power of it was beyond anything I had imagined. In this process of change—leaving my job, selling my car, throttling my lifestyle—came another huge hit. At thirty-eight years old, I realized I had defined myself by my career. I could no longer answer the question, *Who is Sue?* Being deep into the iPEC training and community was perfect timing. It was actually in Module II, during the shuffling game, that this hit me. I wasn't only grieving the loss of parents, I was grieving the loss of self. No, let me restate that: I was grieving the loss of what I *thought* was self. The exciting part was that I was about to find the real one and live it with everything I had. Look out, world!

Accepting a life-altering change was one of the hardest things I've done in my entire life. After struggling, for years, with these issues, I've come to understand that people do not recognize their calling until they evaluate themselves through a process of self-reflection. While examining my current job and measuring my performance among my professional peers, I felt compelled—even forced—to imagine what and where I could be if I would just let go. Letting go gave me the opportunity to find focus from within. Once I realized that I was at my crossroads, I knew there was no looking back; just pushing forward to where I needed to grow.

It took some time to get here, but I am here and embracing the challenges I set forth for myself. As I glance backward, I'm proud of where I came from and what I've deemed accomplished. Back then, I didn't know I was silently preparing myself for this great change, but I feel good for what I've become. We've all been there before: fighting our restlessness and convincing ourselves that this is how it has to be. Is this really what it has to be? Once

"At some point, we let the madness motivate us to cease the madness."

you're filled with all the nonsense you could possibly absorb, trust me: you will be ready for your new pathway. We all feel fear and try to escape it. At some point, we let the madness motivate us to cease the madness. We can face the fear, walk through it and find peace, joy and passion on the other side.

What I have created from this journey is Soaring Solutions, LLC, small-business and life coaching. Yes, a part of me continues down the business path. Here, I get to work with people who choose to evolve and who are motivated to make great change and increase their self-awareness to make their business grow and cultivate happy, empowered employees. The ability to bring together my skill sets in this way is something I never thought possible. On the life coaching side, I focus on health and wellness. My experience in performance dance, endurance running, injury recovery and life-changing eating habits culminated into a passion for helping others work through these goals. And, of course, one of my very deep passions is coaching others through life-changing experiences, to find their true selves, to realize that "this isn't really all life has to be," and break through those limiting beliefs so that they can live their true desire and joy. If you feel a connection to my story, I'd love to hear from you: sue@soaringsolutions.net

I leave you with my favorite quote, sent to me by an amazing woman, Clare Sente, who reached out to me at a Celebrate Your Life Conference. As soon as I made my decision, I saw this in action. It is real—and you, too, can experience this incredible synergy:

> "Until one is committed, there is hesitance; the chance to draw back, always ineffectiveness. Concerning all acts of initiative and creation, there is one elemental truth, the ignorance of which kills countless ideas and splendid plans; that the moment one commits oneself, then Providence moves too. All sorts of things occur to help one that would never have otherwise occurred. A whole stream of events issues from the decision, raising in one's favor all manner of unforeseen incidents and meetings and material assistance which no man could have dreamed could come his way. Whatever you can do or dream, you can begin it. Boldness has genius, power and magic in it. Begin it now."
> —Johann Wolfgang von Goethe

Coaching Academic Creatives

KILIAN KRÖLL

J ust the other weekend, I was sitting in a brightly lit auditorium at Haverford College, ready to start my two-day creative writing workshop with one of my favorites in the world of cartoons and graphic novels. As I'm unpacking my notebook and writing utensils, I'm watching Lynda Barry, with her back to us, lay out, on the three long tables, lined up underneath the chalk board, hundreds of little note cards, which she will use to guide her through her teaching process. Right above her head, she had drawn, with white chalk, a picture of herself with her trademark bandanna and square glasses holding a sign that read, "Please sit anywhere!" A speech bubble on the left said, "Dang!" and the one on the right read, "I'm glad you're here!" After my walk on this wet morning through the Philadelphia suburbs, to my undergraduate alma mater, I felt warmly welcomed. Exclamation marks do it for me every time.

But the welcome was far from over. As sleepy college students, caffeinated middle-aged writers and a couple of former groundskeepers trickled in for the 11 a.m. workshop, Barry turned around to announce that we'd start absolutely on the dot, at 11:15, before she continued laying out her cards. And, sure enough, at 11:14, she makes her way to the back of the auditorium, tells everyone, "You've got one minute to find your seats! Ugh, nope, only fifty seconds... Oh, why, now it's only forty-five... Time to get out your pens and paper!"

This goes on until, at ten seconds before 11:15, she says, "Okay, guys, I'm going to count down from behind the door and then run in like a real teacher on the first day of class." She disappears for a moment, and you hear, "Four…three…two…one!" And she bursts through the door, runs into the classroom, throws her arms out and says to her applauding audience, "Welcome to class, everyone! I'm so glad you're here!"

Creative people teaching in academic settings don't always have this much fun.

In 1997, when I first arrived at Haverford as an international student from Germany and Austria, I was full of curiosity about meeting other smart, interesting and open-minded people from all over the world and taking classes in disciplines I knew little about. I tried out courses in general chemistry and public policy, read Shakespeare for the first time in my life, and joined the choir. I became active in the Lesbian, Gay, Bisexual and Transgender (LGBT) community and gave campus tours to prospective students. I was creative and spontaneous; my occasional cultural confusion leading to many new insights and explorations. I truly enjoyed learning the art of academic writing. I started taking modern dance classes, and I became a social figurehead in the campus community. I let myself be challenged and nourished by this historic institution, and I thrived in it, while also challenging its structures and boundaries. This was my freshman year and nothing could stop me.

By the end of my senior year, in the spring of 2001, I was about to graduate with honors in English, having mastered the art of doing well in my academic discipline. By that time, I had learned how to get the best grades with the least amount of effort. In one of my last senior seminars, my professor handed back my final paper with the written comment: "A+ Fluid & cogent." That's all it said. I didn't even remember what the paper was about. It was then that I knew I had mastered academia in a stupid way: I had traded in my initial intellectual curiosity and creative risk-taking, to attain the status quo of getting good grades. I had not enrolled in that creative writing class or the dance composition seminar, because I wasn't sure whether I could get an A in these subjects I'd never taken. I had given in to implicit institutional pressures, passed down through generations. I graduated as a stifled and uncreative person I didn't recognize.

During the course of rediscovering my curious and creative

self and becoming fully engaged with my surroundings again, I worked on a vegetable farm in northern Virginia, sold books at a gay-and-lesbian bookstore in Philadelphia, went to graduate school in London out of pure intellectual curiosity, returned to Philadelphia to manage the accounts at a nonprofit car-sharing organization, and started to perform on stage as a dancer. Finally, I identified a profession that would engage all my talents and intellectual faculties. So, in the winter of 2006, I decided to become a public school teacher.

There were several things that spoke for the teaching profession, from molding kids in using creative teaching methods to having summers off. I was attracted to teaching because I wanted to apply my intellectual knowledge and intuitive approach to make a difference in poor kids' lives. Also, I believed that my background as a writer and dancer would help me create fun in otherwise deprived classrooms. And, as a person who has lived in many cultures, I felt like I could relate to those who feel misunderstood by and left out of mainstream society. I remembered my own teachers, mostly with fondness, and was struck by the impact they'd had on my life. And, because I felt connected to Philadelphia, I wanted to give back.

So here I was, driven by my idealism to make the world a better place and to experience the full "me" in a profession that would compensate me adequately. After one semester of secondary education classes, I was accepted into a government-supported, fast-track program that selects "highly qualified" individuals who want to teach in the Philadelphia public school system and guarantees them a job with the school district. Because time is tight and the need is great, it trains you to become a teacher in one month and places you in one of the worst-off schools in the city. I felt honored and privileged to have been selected, and I felt energized by the challenge. I was ready to give it my all; to finally have a steady career with good benefits and summers off; to do what I was meant to do.

Thus, my best days as a public school English teacher began. I really loved this teacher-training program! Seriously. Every day for a whole month, I got to learn and grow with sixty amazing individuals, each of them passionate, interesting, creative and accomplished. Not only did we incorporate useful teaching tools into our practice, but we also shared a passion for making a difference and our strategies for how we'd make that work in our respective classrooms. Some people would struggle with their student-teaching assignment and I'd help them see the situation from a different angle; others would support me in my growth.

By the time our month together was over, I had developed many close personal connections, both with my mentors and colleagues, as well as with some of the kids on whom I got to practice my teaching methods. I had helped my new teaching colleagues question their motivations for wanting to teach, strengthen their beliefs in themselves and their students, develop mechanisms to not take their students' behavior personally, and celebrate their little successes along the way. In addition, I questioned

"Run in like a teacher on the first day of class!"

our trainers about why they left the classroom to do teacher training and then helped them to either strengthen their passion for what they were doing, or realize that they wanted to ultimately pursue something entirely different. My underlying message was: *School isn't everything; what else are you doing to help you fulfill your purpose? How can you use the challenges that life has thrown your way to your advantage? What are you willing to change in order to prevent burnout?*

I knew there was a problem when I noticed that I loved the training and supporting my colleagues way better than being in the classroom trying to teach a bunch of rowdy, adolescent boys. In addition, I already yearned for the self-structured summertime before I even entered the institutional life of a dysfunctional, corporate-managed, public school. I also learned that I was more drawn to working with students one-on-one than in large groups, and that I wanted to use my gentle, probing approach much more than a tough, authoritarian one. After just one day as an official public school teacher, I realized that I was in the grips of the same blind ambition I had felt at the end of my college career; an ambition that served the institution more than it served me.

Three years went by before I was formally introduced to the coaching field and, during this time, I collected more evidence for what I love to do. After quitting my job with the Philadelphia School District, I started pursuing my other passions, such as travel, writing and contemporary dance, and ended up working with James Williamson, a choreographer in Philadelphia, to help him produce a large-scale project that he'd been working on over a number of years. Our working process was twofold. On a logistical level, I helped James brainstorm and structure all the details that needed to be in place in order for the production to materialize, ranging from setting rehearsal schedules with eleven dancers, to shuttling sets and costumes between venues, to managing the budget.

On a conceptual level, I probed his ideas for the piece and helped him process his thoughts as he made his dramaturgical decisions. James is an Ivy League-educated creative visionary who prefers to use his right brain to create beautiful and meaningful dance works, but also finds himself teaching as a tenured college professor in a liberal-arts dance department to finance his art. His passion for both intellectual and artistic rigor is what inspired me to contribute to his process.

As part of our preparatory work on the dance production, I suggested we attend an academic conference relevant to the topic of James's art. The conference, titled "Cultural Studies Now," at the University of East London, brought together cultural scholars from around the world, who examine how the arts and social movements influence scholarship and vice versa. Typically, these types of conferences are attended by professors and graduate students who are sent by their respective humanistic and social science departments, but rarely by practicing artists and social activists who work outside the university setting. James and I agreed that we'd both have a unique perspective to bring to this gathering of educators: James, as a professor of dance and practicing choreographer, and I, as a "cultural handyman" with a particular hankering for coaching professional educators and artists alike.

With no intellectual agenda to promote or professional status to uphold at the conference, I was led by my pure curiosity about the research topics, teaching methods and secret passions of the creative academics in attendance; whereas, individuals like James, who are both tenured faculty and practicing artists, were a rare sight at the conference. I did talk to many cultural scholars who were guided into academia by particular creative passions, but who had chosen writing and teaching over artistic production.

What I found were tenured faculty who felt it difficult to step out of their comfort zone of analyzing the world around them and to fully participate in the creative processes that inspire them. I discovered a certain frustration among some about not being able to fully communicate their scholarly passions in their class-rooms, because they felt held back by students and institutions who hold oppositional political views. To my surprise, the feeling of being misunderstood was rampant at this conference full of people who were paid by institutions to, essentially, express their inner beliefs in a highly sophisticated way.

I found that these, and other creative thinkers and practition-ers, including James, often find themselves negotiating their in-ner values and passions for the exchange of resources and rec-ognition from large institutions, such as colleges, universities, arts presenters and charitable foundations. In addition, there is implicit pressure to "please the audience"—be it in a classroom or a theater setting. In addition, there is often a tremendous bureau-cratic effort to make even small advances in making one's vision a reality. With these challenging dynamics at play, it is common to lose sight of one's personal mission and become overwhelmed by extra work, such as cumbersome grant applications and years-long tenure processes—work that is seemingly unrelated to the practitioner's true passion. The result might be an involuntary alignment with other people's or institutions' demands, which may lead to losing sight of one's purpose and early burnout.

I discovered my place at this conference to be reassuring the conference attendees that they are making a critical contribution to the cultural field. Together, we brainstormed effective teaching methods to better reach their diverse sets of students. One pan-elist and attendee at a time, I asked my questions about why they were really here, what they wanted to gain from the conference, what was their most recent professional success, what are their persistent challenges, etc. I challenged the folks I spoke with to see the bigger picture of their presence at their given institutions and to come up with ideas about optimizing their work/life balance. I asked them to set aside their cynicism for a while and open themselves up to transformational experiences. I was sincere and funny, curious and provocative, unselfconscious and easy-going. Their appreciative feedback came in smiles, expressions of relief, and deliberate attempts to follow up with me to share their new perceptions. Even James, a kind-hearted cynic who initially came along simply to augment his academic standing, found creative inspiration in the authentic and critical exchanges with his colleagues. I had the time of my life.

Last spring, after I had traveled, written and danced my heart out, I returned to Philadelphia, once again, and reconnected with my friend from church, Jen, who told me about coaching. "You get to talk to people about their inner passions," she said, "and ask all the questions you want. You get to work with people who are the most interesting and inspiring to you, with whom you connect most easily, and who teach you something in the process. You get to set your own schedule, run your own business, talk on the phone, meet in person, lead groups, teach workshops, travel to conferences. And best of all, you get paid for bringing all that you are to the table and helping others to do the same." I was hooked.

After an extensive search, I enrolled in the premiere coach training program at iPEC. Through the course of my training, I began to understand why coaching found me at this particular point in my creative professional journey. I have gathered my unique skill set in graduate classrooms, dance studios, nonprofit offices, high schools, places of worship, and in four countries on two continents. Now is a time of integrating these experiences into a focused and engaging career.

The coach training with iPEC has allowed me not only to hone my formal and intuitive coaching skills, but also to zoom in on with whom it is that I feel really passionate about working. I've discovered that I have a true fondness for outstanding academic institutions and the creative people who work, teach and learn in them. I also love working with people who make and perform high-impact creative work, be it on stage, in the classroom, from the pulpit, or at professional gatherings. In other words, I help right-brain creative types thrive in the institutions that pay them, and I help them challenge their audiences, students, congregations and professional colleagues in an empowering way. I experience success when I witness people become as authentic, focused, engaging and generous as Lynda Barry running into her applauding classroom to teach the material she absolutely loves for you learn! Exclamation marks and all.

A Legacy
of Love

SAMITA LOOMBA

O n January 5, 1988, my plane landed at Chicago O'Hare and my journey of the American Dream began. It was an entirely new experience for me; not just the studies, but the surroundings, language, culture, eating habits, entertainment, and how people talked, dressed and moved about. What stood out for me, at a very basic level, was cleanliness everywhere. It was a new lifestyle for me. Having grown up in India, in a very protective but progressive environment, this was a major change. I had to very quickly learn that I would have to do housework by myself, and this was not easy at all. I had not learned much about housework because, being the youngest, I was always pampered at home.

The next major thing for me, after landing in Chicago, was joining the university. Filled with excitement and nervousness, I enrolled myself in the Management Information System program in the School of Business at Aurora University. I also joined my first-ever job in the university cafeteria. Being a vegetarian, I realized, within a week, that I wouldn't be able to work there. I moved from the cafeteria to the library, which worked out great for me, because I love to read, and working at the library gave me a chance to meet a lot of people. As I started interacting with others around me, I noticed that nearly everyone was very nice, soft-spoken and helpful. They were very willing to share and show me the ways of the American life.

The university life here was different in certain ways from an Indian university. I felt that the focus of studies here was more practical than theoretical. Even though there was work related to the course, still the pressure was less. Professors were more approachable and willing to help me bridge the gap between the studying styles of two different countries.

Along with the new university life, I was getting myself adjusted to day-to-day living, as well. I was amazed the first time I walked into a mall. I had not seen so many stores together in one building before. Finding out my dress, pant or shirt size was a challenge. The other big thing was to find a vegetarian dish at restaurants. I couldn't initially comprehend why restaurants had such a limited vegetarian variety or just a salad. The good thing was that I was living with my sister, so, at home, food was not an issue.

Oh, I haven't mentioned my family yet. I have a very beautiful, loving, caring, giving and God-loving family. Don't get me wrong; like every other family, we have our ups and downs, but, all in all, the sense that we will always be there for one another is very strong. I lost my father when I was about seven years old, but that loss was just a physical one; his memory was always there. I can still close my eyes anytime and see his smiling face. I very clearly remember the "smile" on my father's face the day he died. I really don't remember much except that there was always a feeling that he loved us all very dearly—not just his immediate family, but people around him, as well. Whenever anyone spoke of my father, it was with respect, and they would talk about how he helped them, one way or the other, and how cheerful, friendly and gentle he was. Their stories gave me a sense of pride and something else, which I will share with you later in my story.

My mother is an extraordinary woman, an educator—very smart, intelligent, confident, loving, giving and caring. Sometimes I wonder whether words can actually do justice to describing her. She is a person who spent all her life—every second of it—taking care of her five kids, making sure that all of us got everything we needed. She never let her own pain, stress, frustration or struggle get in the way of raising her kids. I don't know exactly what happened to her own ambitions or dreams, but we kids became her dream.

I remember those sweet moments when she gathered us around in the kitchen and fed us delicious, warm food. In those days, there were no kitchen tables in India, but we used to have a small, portable clay oven that we gathered around, and she would feed us right there. It is important for me to mention that, no matter how hard life got for my mother, she always made time for helping other people. People came to her often to seek help or advice. She was also very active in volunteering her time for education in human values and religion. She was a very well respected member of the community.

My siblings—one brother and three sisters—are the best. We have our moments of loving, fighting, arguing, crying and laughing together. The important thing is that we are *together*, no matter where we physically reside or how often we make contact. We always have a feeling of comfort and good wishes toward one another. As the youngest, I am at the very advantageous position in the chain of siblings. This means I am pampered and can get away with anything I like and, also, have my siblings do whatever I want them to do for me. Though, I do have to say that, even though I am the youngest, I often find myself in a counseling, mentoring or advising position.

Okay, let's get back to the American Dream. I finished my graduate studies, got married, moved to New Jersey and started working with a telecom company. The work was great, and I enjoyed every bit of it because it was all new knowledge. I always enjoy learning new things, so I am mostly in the mode of asking questions, which can come across to some people as "dumb," but it is what it is. My manager was a very progressive person and helped me get lot of on-the-job training, which motivated me to do the best possible work.

Even though work life was at its best, my new marriage was a roller-coaster ride. Conforming to our Indian culture, I had an arranged marriage, soon finding out that we were two, very different people living under the same roof. We both tried our best to make it work, because the concept of divorce was not as thinkable in our culture; we struggled to make the relationship work. As if that wasn't enough, four years into the marriage, we went through the struggle of having a baby. It was another roller-coaster ride of its own. I cannot fully describe the waves of mistreatment, pain, hopelessness, disappointment, stress and frustration.

Many times, I questioned whether or not was even worth it, but I didn't know how else to handle the situation in which I found myself. On the surface, we did our best to keep everything peaceful, calm and under control, but, deep down, within our hearts, there was ongoing turmoil.

I believe life is like a train ride. Passengers get on, but only a few smile at one another, shake hands or exchange business cards. There is a purpose in each one of those interactions. Similarly, my relationship was a ride in itself and gave me the chance to learn, grow, mature and develop my own vision of life. It got me a step closer to my purpose in life. Sometimes, I questioned the sanity of being in such a painful relationship, even though we had some very beautiful moments. Looking back now, I am convinced that all those experiences were a training ground for me. They helped to shape who I am today, and, in that regard, I am very thankful for those bitter experiences.

My marital journey ended, in 2007, with a divorce, and I moved into a new phase of life, full of possibilities. I was bursting with energy, happiness and liveliness, and I just couldn't stop smiling. I knew that was my second chance at life, to make it whatever I wanted to make it. There were some new things to learn that I had never experienced before. All I had to do was decide which ones I wanted to do first.

Let me take a moment here to clarify something. Even though I was going through different phases of my life, there was one constant feeling: that of wanting to help others. I found myself doing this, especially those in similar situations to ones that I had gone through—my parents taught me well. Earlier in my story, I expressed that, when people shared stories about my father, it gave me a sense of pride. One of the biggest lessons my father taught me was that, when you are gone from this earth, you must leave behind a legacy of love and respect. I heard, saw and felt that respect and love come through other people's stories about my father. They always remembered his good deeds. His lesson stayed with me.

My mother also taught me that, no matter how hard life gets, I must rise above my own needs and be there for others who need me. In addition to my parents, I have a spiritual teacher named

Sri Sathya Sai Baba. He taught me through his actions that service, unconditional love and acceptance of all is the way to live. In my life experiences, I reached a point where my thinking shifted: life wasn't all about me and me alone. There was a strong sense of gratitude for what God gave me in life and a compelling desire to help others the way in which they *need* help from me, not the way in which I *want* to help them. I simply want to be there for them. My prayer to my Higher Coach became, "Make me your instrument of service."

I have two important experiences to share before I get into my coaching life, because they have also contributed to it. Back in 2004, a family member went through a legal battle and I found myself supporting him through it. There is no other way to describe it, but that it was a very scary experience! Since I had never gone through any legal issues in my life, I found myself living a nightmare and constantly worrying about my family members. Sitting in the courtroom, I prayed every second that, somehow, a higher power would intervene and say to the prosecutor, "You are not on the path of truth. This person is not the criminal you make him out to be."

Even though I was praying, the events taking place around me were weakening that prayer, and I slowly started losing faith in the foundation of my own life—the foundation that was built on the principles of honesty, truth and goodness in all. I had many questions about why bad things could happen to good people. I had no answers! For a couple years after that, I really struggled before I was able to make peace with the whole situation. I started praying again and accepting matters as they were showing up in my own life and in the lives of my family members.

Now, to another interesting topic—*dating*—a very different experience full of fun and enjoyment. Remember that I grew up in India, and that dating then was not allowed. So after my divorce in 2007, from my arranged marriage, I had to learn this new skill of dating. What I am discovering is that it is a process of gaining a greater insight into human behavior and insight about yourself and others. It is a process that reveals yourself to you: your strengths, weaknesses, confidence, self-doubts, hopes, dreams, needs, wants and total value system. Surprisingly, the whole process can be very enlightening and empowering.

It is extremely interesting to watch people implement strategies of trial and error. Most people with whom I interact are highly educated and professional, but they are not sure what they are looking for in life—according to them—or in a partner. They are not sure of themselves. What I am curious to know, is how these individuals are feeling about the whole dating process. When I complete my research, I will share it with you. Being part of the process, though, I would like to say that I have nothing but the utmost respect for these individuals.

Dear reader, before we enter into my world of coaching, please, let's pause briefly, take a deep breath and digest the previ-

"There was this feeling that my 'helping' was not complete."

ous chapter of my life. To sum it up, the word that describes my life is *beautiful*. I am very thankful for every thought, event, situation and person who contributed to my life. My reason for sharing specific details of my life is to convey my belief that life can be beautiful, regardless of what comes your way. You can be as happy, in any situation, as you want to be, because there is more to life than the day-to-day thoughts and events. This is also a good point for me to mention that even though I was helping others from time to time, something was missing in my own life. There was this feeling that my "helping" was not complete.

My coaching journey

In December 2008, I was Googling something and the International Coach Federation's link showed up. I don't remember exactly why, but something caught my eye and I clicked on it. As I started reading through it, the words that formed in my mind were, "It is me." I remember saying to myself that this is exactly what I do—something was birthed in me! From that day onward, I started researching information about coaching and, within a month, I had decided to proceed along the path of coaching. At that point, I didn't have much clarity, but it was not needed. I felt that something was propelling me in that direction and I accepted it.

I called iPEC (the Institute for Professional Excellence in Coaching), which was one of the coach training institutions that I had discovered. I was blessed to talk with soft-spoken Deborah Van de Grift, the senior director of a New Jersey school. She explained the iPEC program to me and invited me to attend a conference call regarding the program, with no strings attached. The rest, as they say, is history.

I registered and went to the weekend of the first module, Life Potential Training. I remember the exact thought that came to my mind on the first day of the training: "Yup, I am at the right place." It felt that I had finally found what I was looking for. I met people who were dynamic, energetic, inspiring, radiant, enlightening, spiritual and tenacious. Everyone was eager to learn, share, help and create a very comfortable atmosphere for the others.

For me, the training started at the core—deep cleansing—a chance to probe myself; question my values, thoughts and actions; and determine whether there was alignment between my core being and my outward actions. I realized that, like many people, I had an inner critic who was telling me that I could not do certain things and that I was not good or successful enough. Through the training, I came to a new realization that those gremlins sitting on my shoulders did not need to have any control over my life.

I have always accepted myself as I am, but coaching gave me a chance to normalize that acceptance. I realized that I hold myself to very high value standards and that my self-criticism, in certain situations, was holding me back in life. Letting go of that criticism and accepting the complete human inside allowed me to achieve internal tranquility. When I took the blinders off, I met a beautiful, loving, caring, emotional and nurturing person who is also very organized and goal-, action- and results-oriented. I embraced my new self.

The purpose of coaching for me was not to become a perfect superhuman, but to achieve greater balance and to know how to better apply the choices life presents to me. The training clarified for me that, as a human being, I am going to go through the ups and downs of life, but the important thing to remember is that I have a choice in how I ride that roller coaster.

One of the messages that iPEC conveyed to me is that everything is an opportunity. This resonated with me, because that is how I think about life: it is an opportunity, a game that you decide for yourself how to play. I am not trying to create a rosy picture out of nothing. I am referring to accepting, internalizing and realizing every situation, and then deciding how it presents an opportunity for you.

The prayer that I expressed earlier, "Make me your instrument of service," has now shifted to, "I am your instrument." Coaching is my way of polishing that instrument—myself.

Where I see myself going with my coaching business

My first paying client walked into my life and said that she needed me. She had tears in her eyes and pain in her heart. We spoke for some time and made an appointment to meet.

Each person we meet is our teacher and student—one of iPEC's founding principles that perfectly fits here. We are still working together and, as my client is progressing in her life, she has become my coaching mirror. We are validation of each other's work.

My vision for the business is, "Empowering every individual with tools to reveal and awaken the leader within to its maximum potential."

Executive and leadership coaching is born out of the realization that life is all about leadership. In every aspect of my life—both happy and painful moments—it was leadership, in word, thought and action, that moved me forward. Leadership is not only leading someone else, but also leading your own life, creating your own example of leadership: walking, talking and living that leader.

I am bringing the concept of *leadership coaching* to people with the idea that they don't need *me*—they need *themselves*, and I am a tool that they are going to use to know themselves and realize their dreams. I have created a Leadership Empowerment Program to help them learn and build their own system, in which they can live a very progressive, productive and fulfilled life, as defined by them.

The program also provides training in how to shift the focus from problem to solution. Why focus on a problem? Why not acknowledge it and change it into an opportunity? I have used my situations to figure out what I can learn from them and how I can grow. Isn't life teaching us something every second of our lives whether we are paying attention or not? Through this program, I am sharing a technique that has worked well for myself.

Why not make life fearless? Build a thought system in which there are only solutions and decide where you want to go with those solutions.

A friend introduced me to a song by Yves Larock called "Rise Up," and I love it. *My dream is to fly over the rainbow so high.* I know my purpose and dream today; it has just started and its direction is set. I will limit it if I say, "It's going to go in direction XYZ," so I am just going to fly with it and watch it open doors for me.

From Single and Smoker to Coach and Mom

KARI LOWREY

On December 24 of 2006, I was sitting behind my grandmother in church, trying to mimic the way she was breathing. She was dying of lung disease as a result of many years of smoking. All she could do was gasp for little puffs of breath: in-out, in-out, in-out. It does not take long, breathing like that, before you are light-headed and all you can think about is trying to get more oxygen. What a terrible way to live, yet it was a way of life I was choosing. This is the thought I was trying to get through my head, as I mimicked her breathing: *Choosing to smoke now is the same as choosing to live like this.*

I was a smoker. I was thirty-one years old, and I had been smoking for more than half of my life; a pack a day, or more, sometimes. I'd quit before. Once, I quit for a whole year and, to celebrate, decided I could have just one. Then, I only smoked when I was working in New York. Eventually, I was back to a pack a day. Don't get me wrong; there was nothing wrong with my life. Many people believed I lived an enchanted life. From the outside, my life looked ideal: it included fun adventures, like working with tigers, and living in Argentina. I was a published poet, and I had my master's degree in business administration. I had my dream job as the leadership development trainer for a large corporation, lived in a gated community, and all of my needs, plus some of my desires, were being met.

But I was overweight and a smoker, and I had not been on a second date in more than three years. Although I was successful, I was not happy. As a child, the only real vision I had of my adult life was being a wife and a mother. In fact, my plan had been that I would have my three or four children before I turned thirty. I had no intention of being an old mom. Yet here I was, at thirty-one, still single and childless. Looking at my grandmother, surrounded by her five children, seventeen grandchildren and eleven of her great grandchildren, the thought occurred to me that this was a future I might never have.

Even if I eventually married, the time for having children while I was young enough to watch them have children felt like it was slipping away. My life was happening through a series of unconscious choices that I was making each day, starting the moment that I woke up and lit that first cigarette. No matter how much I wanted a different life, I could not imagine what it would take to get me there. The obvious way to get married and have children would be to date; however, I had a long history of dating tortured souls. Most of the men I had been in relationships with were so caught up in their own drama that my existence was little more than a commercial break. The idea that the choices I was making in my life were attracting those men to me never occurred to me.

On December 26th, my grandmother went into the hospital barely breathing, and I made the decision, again, to quit smoking. She was in intensive care for two weeks, with the family gathered around her. During that time, I felt like I was reprogramming my mind. Looking at the generations of family, thinking, *This is what I want to be, happy and healthy enough to see my children and their children grow up*. Looking at the tubes taking thick, black tar out of her lungs, I thought, *A cigarette now means the tube later*. Many of my other family members were smokers, and they would invite me, each time they slipped outside the hospital to smoke, but no! After two weeks, the machines were turned off, and it was my grandmother who slipped away.

Leaving my family in Ohio, I returned to my life in Florida. Something was different! On a fundamental level, I knew that I had changed. It was not just the smoking, either. My two biggest fears about quitting smoking were that I would gain more weight, and I would never leave my desk at work. For years, I believed those things would happen if I quit. So this time, I did not quit smoking. Instead, I completely changed my lifestyle in a way that smoking no longer made any sense for me. My diet totally changed, and I began eating more fruits and vegetables. Despite having quit smoking, I was losing weight. Smoke breaks were replaced with walking breaks. I felt differently about who I was, my body and my future. My lifestyle changed from carelessness to one of consciousness. It was at this critical moment that I found coaching.

I should say that coaching found me. As a leadership development trainer, I had been "coaching" managers, directors and executives, and I was also training them how to coach their employees. Each time I demonstrated coaching in front of class, participants afterwards would comment that I was a wonderful coach. To build on the skills I had naturally developed, I decided to become a certified professional coach. Through the International Coach Federation, I found a school called the Institute for Professional Excellence in Coaching (iPEC), and they had live classes in the city where I lived. The tuition was expensive, but I knew it was worth every penny, and I was willing to make the investment in myself. I thought, *Even if I never coach a single person, it will be worth it for the personal growth.*

From the moment that I signed up to become a professional coach, my life began dramatically changing. That first weekend, the director of the Florida school pulled me aside and asked if I would be interested in training for iPEC. She and the lead trainer both felt that my ten years of experience as a corporate trainer and my passion for coaching would make me an ideal trainer for iPEC. My Train-the-Trainer program began immediately so that I was simultaneously becoming a certified coach and trainer. It is a journey that changed the course of my life.

My first detour would start on craigslist.com, in the classified section, where people can post under "Men Looking for Women," "Women Looking for Men," etc. Always a curious onlooker for years, I had perused the ads, scrutinizing the way men would try to sell themselves and the pictures they chose. It always seemed silly to me that a man would use a picture of himself, where you can see that his ex-girlfriend had obviously been cut out, to try and find another girl. Self-portraits were another story. Was there no one in their lives whom they could ask to take a photograph of them? Where were their friends?

Kevin's ad was different. It was the story of a man who was looking for a life partner. He talked about himself, showed some photographs, listed some interests, and showed some more photographs. Then towards the bottom he explained, "If you thought that you would never meet someone online then you are probably the woman I am looking for." He continued by describing exactly what he was looking for and what he would not tolerate. He wanted someone who wanted a family, who ate healthily and who took care of herself. He would not tolerate anyone who smoked. At the very bottom of his ad, it explained that he was always on Yahoo Messenger and to instant-message him. I was hooked, and I signed in to Yahoo to send him a message. He was there and we began to chat.

It took less than a week for me to decide to meet Kevin. Our first date was at a Mexican food joint called Moe's. We got along extremely well from the beginning and talked that night for several hours. We went on a second date later that week, and I could tell, by the end of the evening, that Kevin was very interested in me, but I was not sure if I was really interested in him. After all of my bad experiences with relationships, I felt like I needed to know a lot more information about him, very quickly, so that I could make a decision. The next night we were chatting online as we often did, and I began asking him questions.

"There are some things that I need to know about you if we are going to keep dating," I explained as I proceeded with my inquisition. He humored me, answering each question in his own way. That night as I thought over his responses, I decided that we were not compatible for a long-term relationship. So, the next night, I told him that we were going to have to just be friends. He said that was fine, but asked if he could make an observation. Then he said, "No one has ever asked me that many questions, and I think that you asked all of those questions looking for a reason to not date me. And that is okay, but realize that it means most likely you are going to continue to be alone—probably for the rest of your life—because you have already done this for three years."

He was right! As I worked through the situation with my coach, I discovered that my self-defense mechanism, designed to keep me out of bad relationships, was working very well. It was working so well, in fact, that it had kept me from getting into *any* relationship. A relationship is a mirror in which each person can look at him/herself. When you are not ready to see yourself, you will recognize every fault of your partner and work hard to fix them. Fixing them becomes a distraction from taking care of yourself. I was not ready to see or take care of myself.

In my relationships, I tended to choose very unhappy men and I would try to make them happy. The truth was that I only wanted to make them happy to make myself happy. Kevin did not need me to make him happy and he had no intention of making me happy either. I would grow to understand that it is so much easier if both people in a relationship make *themselves* happy. When two people are happy with themselves, they can create a relationship based on common values, interests and desires. It is a very different experience from trying to fix someone or sharing his/her addiction to drama.

It seems easy and obvious, now, to say that, in order to get into a relationship with the type of man I was looking for, I had to,

> *"Change is not difficult, but sustaining changes is hard."*

first, become the type of woman that man would find attractive. I am always telling coaching students, "It sounds simple, but it is not easy." Change is not difficult, but sustaining change is hard. Through the years, I have continued to work with a coach because, periodically, a new situation will arise and my old default, unconscious tendencies will creep up on me. It takes someone outside of me to see that and help me get back to making conscious choices.

What I love most about being a coach is being a mirror and watching others discover themselves, fulfill dreams they've had since they were kids, and find new purpose in their lives. All of this is accomplished through asking them empowering questions.

My clients do not need someone to tell them what to do, rather, someone who will objectively ask them what they are doing. They can do anything they want, as long as they know why they are doing it and believe it is the right thing for them to do at this time. This, I have learned, is the essence of coaching.

In the beginning, I would coach anyone who crossed my path and wanted a coach. Most of my clients were students or referrals from students. They saw me coaching in front of the classroom and felt like I could help them, their friends and family members. My practice had grown to include a diverse group of clients including an artist, a high school teacher and a CEO. Additionally, I had a director who asked me to coach the six managers on her team, individually and as a group. This was a very important experience for me as a coach, because it allowed for me see very clearly which types of clients with whom I was truly energized to work.

My ideal clients are busy professionals, and I help them find balance, engage their energy and connect their achievements to the dreams they had as children. When I receive requests to coach people who are not my ideal client, I refer them out to a large network of coaches I know, consisting of every specialty imaginable. It is extremely important to me that the coaches I train have the tools they need to build successful coaching practices. To support that mission, I have been studying with Michael Port and I am now licensed to train his program "Book Yourself Solid."

Personally and professionally, becoming a coach changed everything for me. Three years later, Kevin and I are now married and have a daughter. I am a work-at-home mom with a thriving coaching practice and I am still a lead trainer and admissions coach for iPEC. There are times that I look around in awe of how my life has changed; how one small shift in my thinking created a completely new reality; not a reality that *happened* to me, but one that I *chose*.

Who Defines Your Success?

JULIE McMANUS

I am a corporate dropout. Up until this point, my life was all about achieving success, money and fame. I never really stopped to define success for *me*. I only desired to achieve some predetermined definition of success. How do you define it? I can only surmise that if you are reading this book, then you probably have a different definition from the one many people hold.

So what is success? For most of us, it is about having an "important title" (V.P., any C title, or Director), making lots of money and to be viewed as successful by others. Have you really taken the time to determine success for *you*? Or are you trying to live up to someone else's definition of success?

I would like to step back some years and take you through my career path. I was in management at a very young age. I made a lot of mistakes and I had a lot of wins. I have spent much of my life trying to make up for those mistakes. I made positive and negative impacts of those around me. I worked hard, though, and was recognized for my hard work and initiative. I was proud of my title, made decent money and felt important; however, I wasn't quite happy. So, I quit.

Fresh out of graduate school, I landed an outstanding consulting job that took me to Australia, New Zealand and throughout the U.S. I loved that job. I had an opportunity to develop training programs for a variety of organizations. As time went on, my job responsibilities were changed and I became unhappy. I could not give my employer 100 percent anymore. One Friday afternoon, I resigned at the Dallas airport.

At the age of thirty-three, I became a vice president of a company. I loved my job and loved the challenges of making a difference, not only in my employees' lives, but in my customers', as well. I made a number of lifelong friends and worked in an area out of my comfort zone. As time passed, I wasn't quite happy, so I gave my notice. I recently left another vice president position. You guessed it: I was unhappy and unfulfilled, so I quit. Are you starting to see a trend?

I hooked up with a coach about a year ago. Not really sure why I did it. I really had never heard of coaching. I just didn't feel good about where I was in life. I guess I thought that the coach would give all the answers. Boy, was I wrong!

> *"I guess I thought that the coach would give all the answers. Boy, was I wrong!"*

My life has dramatically changed as a result of coaching. My definition of success, although not quite complete, has changed, as well. I've learned through coaching and reading that success, for me, was a mask for low self-confidence. If I achieved success, then others wouldn't know I lacked confidence, didn't like myself, didn't feel fulfilled and didn't really want to face myself. In order to really define success for *me*, I learned that I needed to like, and really love, myself before I could ever truly become successful.

What is success? Some would say that I had a very successful career. If so, why was I so unhappy? One of the things that I have learned is that you need to define your own levels of success in order to achieve it. You can listen to what others have to say and try to live up to their expectations, but it will provide you with a false sense of purpose if you live your life trying to live up to those expectations.

I truly believe that, since I have started this journey, I have become more successful than I ever was before. I have become a better listener, a better partner and a better friend. I have done more in the past six months than had I done in numerous years prior. I have been camping three times, had nieces visit for an extended period, learned about myself, lived way outside my comfort zone, thought about things I had never thought about previously, went zip-lining, tried to answer some hard questions, read twelve books, became a role model for people around me, started an exercise routine, lost weight, began hugging people, started a business, took classes, learned to like myself (I am not quite at the love stage yet), crossed fifteen things off my life list, and planned a four-week trip to Africa to do volunteer work.

As I have continued on my journey, I finally realized that I could not serve anyone else, if I couldn't serve myself, first. I know that numerous self-help books tell you these things, but until I started to do it, I didn't quite get it.

Earlier I said that I went to a coach because I felt like I had no alternatives and wanted someone to give me the answers. I was unfulfilled in my life and I wanted someone to tell me why. Well, contrary to what I thought would happen, I found out that the coaching process is not about providing you with the answers. The coaching process is just that—it is a process. It is a process that helps you reach the answers, which are already within you. You may not know this, but you are an amazing being, capable of performing tasks you never thought possible. Deep within, you have answers wanting to emerge, if only you will release them. The coaching process, among other things, helps you to find the answers so desperately sought, which already reside within. The coach helps bring those answers to light.

I have skirted around the definition of success so far, because I don't quite have it finalized yet. I do know, however, that I will define it and I will achieve it. I will no longer work to achieve any preconceived notion of success or allow anyone to define when I get there. This is a very personal choice and one which is well worth the time and effort to address. Why don't you give it a try?

I am in the process of becoming a coach right now. It has been an interesting journey! I have had so many opportunities in my life that can help me to serve others. I believe I can take the PH.D. I have earned in life and help to guide and focus others as they take this most significant journey. I am looking forward to continued growth and learning. I am looking forward to helping others with theirs. I continue to look forward to the journey that is my life!

This year, help me to see the open doors that lie beyond my fears. Help me to believe in that small voice that whispers me toward my dreams.

Let my newly found light become a beacon for those who hesitate in the wings. —Ria Fitzgerald

Feet First

JOURNEY 17

MICHAEL REDDY

Always Successful, Never Fulfilled

It was bittersweet, the day I cleaned out my office. A cold December sky sent pale, gray light through the window. In ten years with the company, I had helped it grow from six employees to near sixty, and to around seven times its original income. So many wonderful people worked there, and our products and services did some real good in the world. The office I was leaving sat in the corner of a beautiful new building, which I had played a significant role in creating. And yet, still…I was not at home in it.

My own characteristic vision for how the larger company ought to be organized and managed seemed to go increasingly unheeded. Playing catch-up to one crisis always appeared, to my mind anyway, to plant the seeds of the next one. The product was awesome, but our delivery, systems, and customer service stumbled too often. Goals for further growth sat hostage, I thought, to runaway complexity and disorganization. I had huge respect for the founder and owner, and in many ways really loved the man— but our views on what was needed to set things right diverged more and more.

And so, I was leaving. And unfortunately that leaving sounded an echo of too many other departures. I could look back on a few decades of adult life and say honestly that I was always very good at what I did—that from the outside, anyway, it always looked like I was a great success. But in my own terms, when it came to my deeper dreams, the inner reality was never that clear.

Behind me was a doctorate from the University of Chicago,

and an assistant professorship at Columbia. The research I had done during that period was actually famous, with the number of hits on Google many years later still running over twenty thousand (search on *conduit metaphor*). And yet I had walked away from that life in anger and conflicted. I had consulted in New York City, made money, and absorbed the high-rolling energy and pace of Manhattan into my blood. Yet two major book efforts had met with uncanny, unhappy, almost inexplicable ends.

I had set out to sail a small boat alone around the world—and found it was not to happen. It seemed like the whole North Atlantic rose up and said, "No way!" Like me—an over-achieving, never-good-enough, oldest son of an alcoholic traveling salesman—my little racing trimaran was too light, too fast, and awfully short on staying power. I was, it seemed, some errant sprinter in a long, hard cross-country race.

Shifting gears entirely, I had apprenticed to Native American elders, and learned their wonderful, earth-based spirituality and healing techniques. As that phase of my life unfolded, I owned and managed a woodworking business by day, while on nights and weekends I led heart circles, sweat lodges, workshops, and vision quests. There was considerable grounding in this for me. I slowed down measurably and repaired, I thought, much of the damage from a difficult upbringing. Woodworking led eventually to doing the interior of the current company's first office, and then to five years as director of organizational development there, and another five as chief technical officer.

But the Native elders who taught and supported me had died. And racial tensions that remained between the white and the red people made it more and more difficult for me to do the Native-American work. Hardliners among the red race felt, perhaps with some cause, that it was wrong for a white man to teach their ways—that their spirituality was an ethnic possession, something they needed exclusively to support their own besieged culture. And so, with profound reluctance and mounting sadness—I had recently walked away from any public teaching or practice of this.

And so there I was, a few days before Christmas, packing books, pictures, and files—at the end of yet another pair of endeavors that had failed to turn out as I would have liked. Well, yes, I had found and taken another job, a very good one too—as the first person hired to set up the Philadelphia office of a growing national technology consulting company. As usual, I would recover, reorient, and hit the ground running. But honestly, the "always successful, never fulfilled" syndrome gnawed ever deeper at my bones. And I had no idea that something completely different was about to happen in my life.

Into the Tunnel
In fact, the really good job I had spent over a year finding and acquiring lasted all of three months. There had been a choice of two positions at the outset, and it seemed like I had taken the wrong one. Being managed from the West Coast as the sole person in a brand-new satellite office also proved cumbersome. Then, the Crash of '08 hit full force—and suddenly the job was no more. Well, I thought I would just live on savings for a while, rest up and sail a lot, and figure out what might come next. I could not have been more wrong.

My feet started to hurt. At first I thought it was just the stress of the previous eighteen months. I got some acupuncture and bodywork, more counseling, and waited for it to ease up. I was in excellent shape, physically. I had eaten carefully and well, worked out, and done yoga for years. There was no reason to think this was anything but a passing phenomenon. But pass it did not. It got worse…and worse.

Eventually diagnosed as "sensory neuropathies"—long flare-ups of stinging, burning, alternating hot or cold pain—started to drive me nuts. No pathology was found to explain them. I didn't like taking drugs in the first place, but even when I was put on stronger painkillers—they had little effect. At their worst, my days became a prolonged effort to endure and find whatever would distract from the hurt. Exercise, walking, sailing, woodwork—anything that involved being on my feet—became harder and harder to do. And the sleepless, pain-filled nights really began to terrorize me.

This kind of neuropathy pain, caused by aberrant signals generated when nerves themselves act up, can be quite strange. Oddly enough, in my case, the only thing that eased it was to have people hold or rub my feet. Real sensations from human hands replaced and shut off the unreal ones, and for a little while, there was peace. On the other hand, old Mr. Independent surely did not like begging people to touch him. My image of this time is that of sitting on my sundeck, furiously carving wood to distract myself, and lining up friends to come by and hold my feet.

But I was sinking…furious that nothing—including one serious prescription drug that made a zombie out of me—seemed to be able to cure or even manage this. This also seemed true for a lengthening list of alternative healing modalities. Mounting anxiety about not being able to endure the next flare-up of foot pain was certainly compounding the problem. As my view of all this grew darker, it seemed that, in much the same way that so many things had not worked out for me, my entire useful life was now collapsing. There I sat, having done for decades all the right things for my health—and now once again saddled with uncanny, perverse, debilitating results.

A Light in the Darkness—Constellation Work

Eventually, over six months from onset, it was clear that therapy, supplements, acupuncture, bodywork, homeopathy, and an experimental immune-system treatment were not shifting anything. They certainly helped me endure it and keep searching—but nothing seemed to really turn the corner. The normal allopathic doctors, with their expensive tests, still found nothing significantly wrong. They could only offer drugs whose impact was small and side effects on me were really noxious.

I worked constantly to exercise however I could, to auto-suggest healing and recovery to my subconscious, and to be open and listening for what it was I might need to learn from this. But these all seemed to provide about enough strength and insight to keep me going to suffer more. It was at this point, running out of things to pin the next hope upon, that I bought a book by John Payne, called *The Language of the Soul*.

What I read in it was an explanation of something developed over the last twenty years in Germany called "constellation work." The stories this book told were about people "entangled" with the unaccepted fates and feelings of their recent ancestors.

Their suffering was, in essence, not so much an individual issue, but rather a condition of their membership in the family group, a matter of misplaced love or loyaltiy.

It spoke of family systems, or "family souls," that, in their effort to survive intact, performed a kind of load balancing—literally distributing trauma across generations. What was too much for one to bear, another who came later would share. Otherwise, the family would have suffered a worse fate, it seemed, or died out entirely—and that later one might not have been born.

Apparently a German named Bert Hellinger had developed a method for revealing and releasing these entanglements. As I digested these ideas, something clicked in me. Oh, my God—didn't I remember my mother telling me some story about how my father had had terrible problems with his feet in World War II? As the possibilities of this perspective for my own life fell into place, I plunged, with very real urgency, into the constellation process. I found Andrea Bosbach, a German-trained practitioner in Philadelphia, and also signed up to go down to South Carolina for a weekend with the author John Payne.

This work is done in several ways, but the most amazing and dramatic is in workshops. After a brief statement of "the issue" and some questions about background from the facilitator, the client stands strangers up intuitively in the room to represent relevant members of the ancestral family. Most of the time, if they are left in silence for a few minutes, the representatives' body language and emotional reactions to one another begin to mirror the dynamic that exists in the family group.

As the "systemic" relationships become clear, the facilitator can begin helping entangled ancestors, through their representatives, to take back their own fates and feelings. These then will usually turn towards the client and offer support for letting go of the hidden loyalties that anchor unhappy conditions. Sometimes this triggers complete relief. Other times it means that remedies that failed previously now start to work.

So the healing here, the reframing, applies to the whole family system—not simply to the client. Yes, it does somehow seem to affect whatever is left of the dead. Whether that happens only in terms of the memories or epigenetic material of the living, or more broadly via some sort of "paranormal" field effect, remains at this point an open question. What is not in question is this—diseases, chronic conditions or problems, mysteriously persistent failures of almost every kind have been changed for the better with this approach. Sometimes, it appears, perhaps more often than we think, our suffering is not simply our own. (For further explanations, see www.reddyworks.com.)

Loyal to the Lost

As I moved into the first couple of months of this work, two things happened to me. One was, I knew very quickly that, if I got well again, I wanted to learn to facilitate it myself. Not only was this utterly fascinating, but it seemed to be the natural extension of my years of Native-American practice. Indeed, the racially oriented natives were always telling us white "wannabes" to go connect with our own ancestors and leave their red heritage alone. In a miraculous and unexpected way, in learning to lead this work, that is exactly what I would be doing.

But the second thing that occurred was little short of a miracle. I became aware of and started to unload the rather large amount of my family's trauma I had been carrying unconsciously all my life. Loyalties that had bound me to the "never-fulfilled" patterns emerged crystal-clear in my constellations. I experienced complete strangers speaking somehow for my ancestors and telling me to give these things back to them and to be well and thrive in my own life. And, as my family system rearranged itself, finally the pain in my feet started to subside. Hallelujah!

On the one hand, I was amazed and hugely grateful. At the same time, it tended to rock my worldview, since I thought I had rejected my birth family and left them entirely behind. Was it really true that such an approach typically only blinds you to your underlying loyalties? The hard evidence was staring me in the face—or rather, the feet.

Though he never talked about the war, from my mother I know that my father fought first in the Aleutian Islands, off Alaska. There he got scurvy from bad food and froze his feet. Shipped back to the states for Officers Candidate School, he still had abscesses on them. Not wanting to be "washed out," he never told anyone about them. Instead he snuck into the bathroom in the middle of the night, drained, washed, and re-bandaged the abscesses, and went on with the twenty-mile hikes.

Then, he took part in the battle for Okinawa. This was a monumental eighty-two-day horror in which a hundred thousand Japanese troops were killed, fifty thousand Americans wounded, and one-quarter of the civilian population either died or committed suicide. But the atomic bombs were dropped a couple of weeks later and, *well, gosh, sorry—looks like we didn't need to take that island after all. Never mind.* Picture young men ripped out of college, sent through something like this, and then expected to come home and "just be normal." They were not. My dad packed it all away somewhere inside and took to drink.

From the family-systems perspective, in terms of my feet, and my inexplicable descent into a pit of pain and anxiety—everything was quite clear. What dad could not acknowledge, I took in, carried through my life, and found at different times various ways to feel for him. What happened to me after leaving the company had all the earmarks of an intense episode of post traumatic stress disorder (PTSD). Which actually belonged to my dad. And then there was his survivor guilt. Sometimes people see too many humans, some very dear to them, utterly destroyed, and are not able to come to terms with this. Typically, such survivors sabotage their own success in life. *How can I do well, when so many brothers were slaughtered?*

Turning around, at this point, looking back over places and times in my life where, despite talent and determined effort, things went really wrong for me—for the first time I started to understand. I had always resonated at some very deep level with the "have nots." And a major source of that resonance was not so much my own feelings, but rather my father's deep connection to all the lost souls in his terrible war experience.

Out the Other Side—iPEC Coaching

Deep changes come very often in waves. The trend is upward, to be sure, but there are still some scary downturns to move through. On the one hand, I had not merely understanding and new hope, but also real changes in my feet to buoy me up. On the other, the months of fear, pain, anxiety, and constant stress still had me on an emotional and metabolic roller coaster. I was fragile, physically weak, still quite frightened, and largely unable to sleep.

Yes, I had discovered something amazing and maybe I was not going to be crippled. But no, after the collapse I had experienced, that alone was not going to regenerate an outgoing, positive personality and a happy, now genuinely fulfilled life. Was I really going to get well and strong again? Or was this just a mirage in the desert? I felt I needed some sort of serious recovery or retraining program.

At Christmas, one astonishing year after packing my office and departing the company, I was able to fly west and see my aging mother. During that visit, listening to her tell me recollections of the family she had known—with me for the first time actually interested in them—I remembered something else. A long time before, when I was in college and my father was just drying out, he gave me a book by Maxwell Maltz called *Psycho-Cybernetics*. That book kindled in me a lifelong interest in auto-hypnosis, meditation, affirmations, the power of positive thinking—all the ways in which we might enlist the power of the subconscious mind in creating our lives.

Over the years I had read constantly and done many trainings, the ESTs and Silva Mind Controls of the times, that approached this in various ways. Even in the depths of my recent pain-filled months, I had taken whatever my worst fear of the week was, recorded an affirmation out of its opposite, and played that to myself through headphones at night. I have no doubt that helped me survive and keep searching. Maybe this was also the way to grow a new self from the wreckage. After all, with everything in shambles, was there not now the maximum amount of clear space to redesign, to rebuild?

On my mother's old Macintosh I started an Internet search. If there was a current reincarnation of positive, forward-looking, solution-focused methods, it seemed they had now taken the form of "coaching." I had so much experience, maybe I should become one of those—a coach. I looked at several programs, made some calls, and ended up talking to Deborah Van de Grift at the Institute for Professional Excellence in Coaching (iPEC). It looked like a serious training program for both life and business coaches. Deborah seemed both grounded and positive, and was clearly evaluating me—just as I was sizing up her responses and iPEC's offering. In the last days of the old year, I signed up.

Looking back, I can only say, if there were two new feet for a new me to walk on, and one was constellation work, then the other, just as certainly, was the wonderful training and amazing support from iPEC's coach-training program.

Why do I say that? Well, many of the principles, practices, ideas, and methods that iPEC teaches were not new to me. I had seen them, used them, and even taught some of them before. What I had never seen was all of them brought together into one coherent package. In fact, that package was seriously synergistic. The whole was really greater than the sum of the parts. And the other element, a really key element, was the power of a two-person partnership—as opposed to trying to do all these things on one's own.

One of the ways I now market my coaching services is to encourage people to self-coach using various techniques. I give them away in a magazine column and blog I write for called "Coach Thyself" (*see* www.reddyworks.com). Doing this is a

> *"iPEC's Core Energy Coaching is a unique, dynamic, self-empowering relationship"*

win/win proposition. If people use them on themselves, they will get real value. But the value they will get from having the professional, dedicated, experienced support of a coaching partnership is easily four or five times greater. All good coaches have gotten this truth, and have coaches themselves.

iPEC's Core Energy Coaching™ process is a unique, dynamic, self-empowering relationship—one that's a little hard to describe. Most people have never experienced anything like it. And I'm not certain the term "coaching" does it justice. Let me explain it with a question. What do you think starts to happen in the lives of motivated people, when they have at their side someone who:

Has only one agenda—to see them thrive in life and career;

Always listens, validates, and supports their reality, their experience;

Believes they know best—that the best answers come from within them;

Helps clarify what they really want using professional techniques;

Brainstorms with them to design solutions, and think outside of their box;

Uses professional planning skills to lay out balanced, achievable goals;

Holds them accountable to take the steps they say they will;

Helps them bypass blocks with professional tools if these stand in the way?

Have you personally ever been the focus of this kind of attention? Honestly, done right, it's a positive, synergistic whirlwind. Most people experience extraordinary, sustainable results. And though they may be busy, a deep connection to their true passions makes those activities feel effortless.

The results in my case were just exactly the steady recovery and rebirth I was looking for. For the better part of a year, immersed in studying and mastering these techniques, practicing coaching on peers and early clients, with the support of coaches who were either part of the program, or hired by me—out of the ashes of the old Michael, I really did put together a brand-new self. For this self, the old Native-American night job (helping people find themselves) that was deeply aligned with my passions finally has become my day job.

I simply cannot express how happy this has made me. All the experience and knowledge of the old self remains at my fingertips. But so much of the pain and empathic suffering for ancestors caught up in the horrors of a war I never experienced—that has dropped further and further away. Beyond that, as someone who already knows a lot about small businesses, I can say that the support that iPEC gives its graduating coaches for really getting a coaching business going is simply superb.

Is every day somehow perfect now? No. I have, like all of us, my ups and downs, my characteristic strengths and weak spots.

But I look back on a dark night of the soul that was truly horrible—and it feels like an old, faded, vanishing bad dream. I think of my father, and instead of rejection and hatred, I feel mutual warmth, understanding, and support. And as terrible as the experience really was, honestly, from my heart, I can say that Bruce Schneider is right—the bigger the challenge, the richer the opportunity. I faced some really terrible dragons—but look what they were guarding. A most amazing pair of treasures! Two powerful new tools! A whole new life! What a magical outcome!

The Mission of ReddyWorks

You know what's even more magical? What's even more magical is that I'm now using these tools to guide individuals and businesses through their own transformative experiences. That goes on every day now. Of course, in realizing their dreams, most do not go through anything like the kind of crisis that emerged for me. Let's keep that in mind. But a few do, and either way, I know the terrain.

My current business combines the two new perspectives of professional Core Energy Coaching and systemic constellation work. With this unique blend of cutting-edge tools, considerable experience in business operations and systems, a certification to teach Michael Port's "Book Yourself Solid" marketing methods, and another one from iPEC to deliver Energy Leadership assessments—ReddyWorks is becoming a one-stop shop for creative individuals, wellness professionals, and entrepreneurs. We help them transform challenges like chronic disease, family conflict, and business instability (too much, too little) into opportunities for vibrant growth.

Here's how coaching and constellation work complement each other. Coaching moves all serious clients forward. If they come up against blocks, and these are on the individual level, iPEC's Core Energy Coaching has wonderful methods for removing them, or even turning them into allies. But in my partnerships, we also keep an eye out for blocks that are not simply an individual issue—that arise from not-so-conscious loyalties clients may hold to families or businesses. These do not yield so easily, or yield but recur. For these we turn to constellation work.

Others come first to constellation work. They have discovered an emerging need to look into and shift the roles they play in groups that are crucial to them. Something is happening to them, or their children, or other relatives that seems persistent, problematic, out of character for the individual, or mysteriously difficult to resolve. Often, when we reveal and re-align the entangling dynamic with the group, then some coaching helps them ground and actualize the changes in their lives or businesses. The two perspectives are wonderfully complementary. Both are forward-looking, solution-oriented, and visit the past only long enough to reframe it—to not only see, but also feel it differently.

One of my central passions is helping coaches, alternative-healing professionals, and wellness entrepreneurs add the family systems perspective to their toolset. "Family souls," whether in ancestral groups or businesses, tend to follow certain patterns in the way they balance things out. Training in facilitating constellations is not necessary to understand these patterns and begin to look for them when clients hit real roadblocks. The ability to distinguish individual issues from likely group-level loyalties, knowing when to perhaps refer someone for a constellation—these can measurably increase the efficacy of one's coaching or healing practice.

There's Gotta Be a Way

DEBORAH SAKELARIS

My life prior to coaching

Growing up a Midwesterner, I learned the value of a dollar, commitment, stability and the importance of family, right from the beginning of my life. I was born and raised in Munster, Indiana, a small Midwestern town thirty-five miles from downtown Chicago on the edges of the steel-mill industry. I have one older brother, Jeff, and everyone with whom we grew up, in our neighborhood, was pretty much just like us, with two-parent households. Moms stayed at home until the kids could be trusted not to beat each other up and get into trouble. Dads went off to work in the steel mills, which was a booming business at that time. Friends and family were always around. Dinner was at 6 p.m., with everyone around the table talking about his/her day. The dog was always begging for food or wanting to play. Church was attended, on a weekly basis, and life was good.

When I think back to that time, some of my fondest memories are of celebrations. My mom made sure that every birthday, holiday and special occasion was celebrated in great style. I loved those celebrations, and I have carried on that tradition in my adult life today. I celebrate everything—just ask my husband! Oprah Winfrey once said, "The more you praise and celebrate your life, the more there is in life to celebrate." I couldn't agree more!

Growing up Irish Catholic and being part Romanian, there were a lot of traditions brought into our world. Corned beef and cabbage were always served on St. Patrick's Day, and my Grandma Kovan made the best *plachintas* (Romanian crepes). My dad is the Irish one, Charles O'Donnell, and my mom the Romanian one, Darlene Kovan. My mom instilled the importance of attending church services on a weekly, and, sometimes daily, basis, and she gave me the foundation for my religion, spirituality and relationship with God. This early foundation weaved its way throughout my life, has sustained me through difficult times and made me the woman I am today.

As I worked my way into high school, I learned about change and how to very quickly handle it, as new friends were made, boyfriends came along and life started to get a little more complicated. Throughout those four years, I joined everything, including track, gymnastics, volleyball and cheerleading. There is where I really learned the value of teamwork at a young age, and I would say that those lessons learned in high school taught me to be a great team player, in all areas of my life.

Being from that small town in Indiana, everyone knew that they were going to go to college; it wasn't really an option. You were expected to go and make a better life for yourself, be self-sufficient and find a great career. I attended Ball State University in Muncie, another small town, four hours south of my home town. College was a fabulous experience. My roommate was Monica Denney. She and I were inseparable, and she was, actually, the daughter of my mom's good high-school friend, Monica Mika, who has since passed away. Monica and I met shopping for prom dresses and the rest is history. We are still very connected, and I am actually the godmother of her son Lukas.

During these college years, Monica and I adopted a saying, "There's gotta be a way!" We said this whenever we were facing any challenge in our life, whether a serious challenge or something fun like getting into a Bruce Springsteen concert. I have loved his music since *Born to Run* came out.

Another part of my college life was being a resident assistant (RA). What an experience! Great skills were learned in this role, including learning how to manage peers, organizing, program development, team-building, and customer service. I also had my first experience of overseas travel during the first quarter of my junior year, when I studied at Regents College in London and traveled all over Europe. I remember negotiating with my parents about helping me pay for this experience. I bartered being an RA for my senior year for their help in financing this study-abroad program. Negotiation skills were always a key asset to have, especially in college, and they serve me well in my current adult life.

One other great aspect of growing up and being on my own, was that I became friends with my parents and no longer had just the child/parent relationship. Reliving another Springsteen concert, I took my mom to see Bruce for her fiftieth birthday, in my senior year. It was like hanging out with my best girlfriend and we had so much fun! My mom and I still feel like we are "Born To Run!"

At Ball State, I studied and received my B.S. degree in journalism. I thought, for sure, I would be a writer or a reporter; however, after college, I headed to Disney World. That is a truly magical place or, as Disney states, "The Happiest Place on Earth." My mom drove me down to Florida, and I will never forget how sad we both were when she left. I was so far away from home and had to really trust my faith that everything was going to be okay in the land of Mickey Mouse.

I started out as a tour guide in guest relations at the Magic Kingdom and then, at the Disney MGM Studios, and it was there that I realized I had a real passion for teaching and training. From guest relations, I moved into the executive suite working for the president, and I was able to really see how the parks worked and what it took to make a great company. The Disney culture is something to experience, especially from the inside. Their training program is the most extensive and most amazing process to experience, and their idea of great customer service should be spread into every company and organization in the world.

It was during my time in Florida that I realized I wanted to be in some kind of training-and-development role in my career. I had a deep-down love for helping people, showing them new and exciting things, and creating joy and happiness in their lives. As I worked in Orlando, made great friends, and had more fun than should be allowed, I realized I needed something more. *Something was missing!* My family was hundreds of miles away, back in

Indiana, and I didn't feel settled in Fantasy Land. I was really searching for some meaning and purpose in my life. I didn't really know what to do, so I did some soul-searching and decided it was time to leave Florida and return to school to acquire new skills and create a new life path for myself.

I had heard about this field of wellness and it resonated with me. So, a year later, I found myself back in Muncie, enrolled in the Ball State University graduate program for Wellness Management. I put myself through graduate school by being a resident hall director. I lived in the hall with all of the underclassmen, and I can remember how great it was to be back on a campus, working with excited students.

Upon completing my master's degree, I ventured back to my home town of Munster and became the Director of Wellness for the Wellness Council of Northwest Indiana. I was very happy to be back home and close to my family.

At the Wellness Council, I was able to make a big impact in people's lives. I loved it and truly felt a great passion for what I was doing. I was working with steel-mill employees, hospital staff, and several other corporations, training them on weight management, smoking cessation, and stress management, as well as presenting on topics around social, occupational, spiritual, physical, intellectual, and emotional health and wellness. I was truly enjoying the journey I was on at that time.

Three years into my career at the Wellness Council, which was a nonprofit organization, the Council lost its funding and, of course, the next step was to cut out the staff. So there I was, a master's degree in hand and out of work. I was determined not to move back home with my parents. As much as I love them, living with them after a certain age is stressful for everyone! So, as I pursued wellness- and health-promotion jobs, I took on any temp job that would come my way. I started to get discouraged, as I wasn't finding anything that I liked in the wellness field.

At this time, one of the managers at the temp agency with which I was registered, asked me if I'd ever thought about being a recruiter. Of course, no one really thinks about being a recruiter, and there is no recruiter degree, but I thought this was something I could do for a year, if I had to. The job was in downtown Chicago. I did always want to work in Chicago, but I wasn't sure I was ready to do the three-hour roundtrip commute every day. Nevertheless, I decided I *had* to be ready, and I took that job. I took the job as a recruit. Seven company-name changes and three different positions later, eleven years had flown by. I had been a recruiter and a sales person, and, finally, my last position with Randstad was managing the Franchise Division. I absolutely loved that job. I was able to travel all over the country, training franchise owners and their staff members on the business, as well as doing some team-building and leadership-development workshops.

Each one of the owners was unique. There was Carolynn Buchanan in Gainesville, Florida. She was the ultimate believer and had the most amazing faith. No matter what came her way, she new the Lord was on her side and nothing could stop her from being successful. Then there was Heather Rafferty, in Albany New York. She was a fireball. Nothing got in her way, but if it did, she moved it out of her way pretty quickly. And also Steve Conine in Reno, NV. He brought a great business mind to the table and was able to invigorate the entire franchise group when he joined the team. There were so many more people—too many to mention here—but they all taught me so much, and I am thankful that I was able to have that experience; I wouldn't trade it for anything. I still stay in contact with the above-mentioned owners, and I still love to be inspired by what they are doing with their businesses.

While I was in that job, I decided it was time to live in the city, so I left my home in Indiana and moved into a condo with my friend, Patrick. He was strictly a friend and, once again, I said, *I could live with this person for a year and then I'll find something else.* Well, timing doesn't seem to actually work out the way we plan it, and I ended up living there for five years before I met my husband and moved a block a way. Living in a big city like Chicago is fascinating. It has been a wonderful experience, and I have made some of my best friends, who are actually like family to me.

What led me to coaching
While I was managing the Franchise Group for Randstad, I had

started to learn more about this new profession called coaching—and not athletic coaching, but business and life coaching. I decided to pursue coach training at the Coaches Training Institute. Timing is everything! Right as I was finishing up my training, Randstad had decided that all of the managers needed to live in Atlanta. There was no way I was moving to Georgia; Sweet Home Chicago is where I was going to stay.

I wasn't sure where I was going with Randstad, even before the management decision to move everyone. So, I decided to do some self-development and test my abilities outside of the work

"I started to try things I'd never done before and take some risks in life."

environment. I started to try things I'd never done before and take some risks in life—really stretch myself! I remember reading a quote by John F. Kennedy that said, "Conformity is the jailer of freedom and the enemy of growth." I was ready to grow and not conform! Next thing I knew, I was registered to run the Chicago Marathon. From that experience, I learned that many things we do in life are like running the marathon and we each have to find our own formula that works best for us, whether running a marathon or running our lives.

I still wanted to stretch and explore new things in life, so I decided to go to Romania with Habitat for Humanity and build houses. After this, I had discovered that we are a truly blessed country and that I am an extremely blessed woman; also, that I am a good carpenter! After those fabulous life experiences, I decided to let go of past expectations and just live my life. Once I did that, things started to happen. I met the man of my dreams and, within ten months, I married my husband, Jim. What a whirlwind it has been!

We started our life together in Fiji, where we spent our honeymoon. Upon returning, that first year, I had many transitions in my life. Not only did I get married, I became a stepmom to twin eight-year-old children, Isabelle and Ben, and left my job at Randstad. I decided to start a coaching practice, moved, gutted a condo while living in it, and tried to decide whether I was doing all the right things to get me to where I wanted to be in life.

I was very happy to be married. Jim and I traveled and enjoyed our life together seeing places like Anguilla, the British West Indies and Ireland, as well as several places in the States. I was nervous about leaving Corporate America but knew it was time to find my new career. This was quite challenging, as I was at Randstad for so long that I couldn't imagine being anywhere else. But when it came time to leave, I took the severance and I started my coaching business, Rodas Coaching. *Rodas* is a Celtic word meaning door. I thought opening doors was exactly what coaching did for people, so I decided my tag line was going to be, "Opening doors to success in business and in life."

What iPEC training has done in and through my life

I ran my business out of my downtown-Chicago office, which is a fabulous location across the street from the Sears Tower. After two years, once again, I found myself missing something. At this time, my coaching focus was on working with people in life transitions and work/life balance issues; however, I needed more and wanted to give more. That was when I discovered iPEC, the Institute for Professional Excellence in Coaching.

iPEC has been the greatest thing I could have ever done for myself and my coaching career. The coach training I received at iPEC reaffirmed my passion of being a coach and gave me amazing tools to do it a thousand times better than I was doing it in the past. The in-person training modules, the teleclasses, the peer coaching, the bookreading and the mentor coaching were all excellent, and all gave me new ways to look at myself and my business. All of the new people who have come in to my life through iPEC are *amazing*, strong, smart, beautiful people whom I am proud to say I know. Many of us from my class have stayed in contact, and they have all enriched my life. This was an exciting outcome, above and beyond the actual training. Now that I am certified through iPEC, not only in their Core Energy Coaching™, but also in their Energy Leadership Coaching, I am more productive, profitable and passionate every single day.

The future of my coaching business is going to be to let people know that I am a professional, certified coach with expertise in life transitions, work/life-balance issues and the Energy Leadership Development system. I have over twenty years of training experience and will continue to offer workshops, teleclasses, group coaching and one-on-one coaching. I will always look for new and exciting ways to create an excellent and superior coaching experience for my clients. I am thrilled to be a part of an industry that is thriving and on the cutting edge of something wonderful in this world. Through my journey, I have come to realize that life is what we make of it.

The future belongs to those that believe in the beauty of their dreams. —Eleanor Roosevelt

I am blessed to have the life I've created, and I know that if I live by my values, stay passionate and continue to make a difference in this world every single day, I will be living the life of abundance that I was meant to live.

Therefore I say unto you, what things soever ye desire, when ye pray, believe that ye receive them, and ye shall have them." —*Mark*, 11:24

Living your dreams means taking action. Join me on this journey by connecting with deborah@rodascoaching.com and create the life of your dreams!

Carol the Coach

CAROL JUERGENSEN SHEETS

My story's intention is to demonstrate three life lessons that I found invaluable while on my journey to becoming a coach and being a coach: 1) no matter what happens to you, you must never give up; 2) pay attention when doors open and have faith that they will take you exactly where you need to go; and 3) believe in yourself and know that you can accomplish anything...one step at a time.

Here is my story; it will hopefully motivate you to follow your dreams and have faith that the rest will come.

I have been a psychotherapist for over thirty years, but what I realized, in the year 2000, was that I wanted to take my life to the next level and reach more people in their quest to live their best lives. So, as a result, I shared, with the medical director for whom I worked, my larger-than-life goals to: write a book, have a weekly segment on the news, and have a radio show on which I could assist others in actualizing their potential.

My supervisor shook his head, knowingly, and asked me how I planned to accomplish such lofty goals. I told him that I was going to solicit each radio and television station in the area and sell myself and my services. He said that he would support me in any way possible, but I could see on his face that he thought my goal would not likely be achieved. I suspect that he had a limiting belief about a forty-four-year-old social worker impacting the world by having her own radio or television show.

I sent out contact information, shared my vision with all the radio and television program directors in the city, and waited to be contacted, to no avail. Then, I contacted a friend's son who was a broadcasting student at the local high school and asked him if he could help me. He agreed that he would make me a radio demo tape and we set the date to do the taping. I showed up with my girlfriends, who had real life problems, and, with the flip of a switch, he was able to make the tape sound like two callers needing some expert advice.

Create and then wait

Five days later I had the demo and was sending copies out to the thirty-two radio stations within a one-hundred-mile radius. I felt so good mailing them out that I could not wait for the responses. I assumed that it would take at least three weeks to get a response, as I knew the program directors would likely be very busy.

I waited and I waited, but received no responses. So I followed up by calling every program director, leaving each one a message. Still, I received no calls back.

That is okay, I told myself, *in sales you must hear thirty no's to get one yes.* So I sent out another batch for Round Two and patiently waited for the fallout. After another three weeks filled with no responses, I decided to find another way to get my message out. I sent my demo to our local paper in hopes of securing a reply.

Doing something different to get different results

Finally, I received a response from the paper, wanting to know my intention. They asked me what I hoped to accomplish, and I responded that I wanted to be the local Ann Landers, to which they replied, "Carol, we have an Ann Landers." *Hmm*, I thought, and then they asked me if I had ever heard of life coaching. Well, the truth of the matter is that life coaching had intrigued me, and I had just signed up to attend a two-day coaching seminar. I embellished and said, "Why, I am in training to be a personal life coach." I mean, I had just signed up for the training, so I felt justified in saying that I was in training. They then asked if I had ever published. Because I had published a two-paragraph summary for our national association publication and realized that this would not get me a column in the paper, again I embellished (not lied), but said, "Why, yes, I have." They responded by asking me to send them my previously published material. When I hung up the phone my heart was racing, because I knew that the two-paragraph summary was not going to get me the job. So what did I do?

I went to the library and took out eleven books on coaching, writing three columns that I thought would be pertinent to coaching. I sent them a column on what a personal life coach did, a column on the five primary feelings and how identifying them helps you to be more authentic, and a column on how you have to find happiness in who you are, despite the changes you want to make. I signed each one of them "Carol the Coach" and sent them off to the paper. One week later, they called to have me come in for an interview. When I got to a building that was three blocks long, I felt a powerful sense of confidence as the editor introduced me as Carol the Coach to many of the staff.

When we sat down, she reached across the table and said, "Carol, these columns are exactly what we want and our only regret is that we cannot use this previously published material." You can imagine how pleased and surprised she was when I said, "Ah, but yes, you can use them as I customized them specifically for you!"

"Carol the Coach" was born

And that was the start of my self-taught coaching career and my desire to inspire large groups. The paper had approximately eight hundred thousand readers, and I very quickly became the go-to person to learn how to reach your goals, achieve success, create your dreams or live an authentic life. It was exactly what I needed to create the brand and the expertise to sell myself on radio and television—and within a year. I sent out those same demo tapes with a new label that branded the show as *The Carol the Coach Show* and was immediately picked up on a local news/talk station looking for programming on Sundays. It was the perfect opportunity to learn the ropes and define my skills.

When that show ended, I moved on to the biggest radio talk station, and, later, I was picked up for a two-hour radio show. Currently, I do a three-and-a-half-minute segment, "Life Skills with Carol the Coach," on the largest local television station in Indianapolis, promoting the foundation principles upon which iPEC's certification is based.

A serendipitous event

That is the other exciting part of the story. You see, I had told *The Indianapolis Star* that I was in training to be a coach because I had just signed up for a two-day seminar on coaching, but five days before the seminar was to start, September 11th happened. It closed down the airports for several days, so the workshop was cancelled. I knew that I needed to get training, but did not know what school would be best for me. As I investigated the many schools that offered coach training, I quickly realized that iPEC offered the best training based on my background and experience. It had a psychological bent that would help me in my work with clients, and yet it clearly emphasized an iPEC principle: "the client has all the answers within." Something as horrific as 911 resulted in a better choice for coach training.

iPEC was the perfect fit for me! And it would not have occurred if I had been the local Ann Landers, or if I had not signed up for that first coaching workshop, or if I had not started to brand myself as Carol the Coach. Although I know that you don't have to be certified to be a coach, I knew in my head, heart and gut that I was calling myself a coach and would benefit from an accreditation program that nurtured my gifts and talents. I also believed that if I was going to call myself a coach, I needed to have all the skills and foundation principles to pass on to the client. From day one, I knew that iPEC training would make me a better person and a better coach. As iPEC's motto says, it is all

"The energy I receive from my clients is very replenishing!"

about "raising the consciousness of the world one person at a time," and that means it had to start with me.

What I know to be true, is that each person has so many gifts inside that are meant for the greater good of human kind, and coaching allows a person to navigate through his/her daily life to access those gifts. As a psychotherapist, I worked on healing the wounds, and as a coach I work with clients who want to activate their strengths to make the world a better place. I also love a profession that empowers me when I empower others. The energy I receive from my clients is very replenishing! It is always a win/win proposition!

When I do keynotes and workshops, I reveal how I embellished my publishing endeavors and training, which did not initially occur as a result of 911, but I didn't outright lie. You see, I knew I had a mission to make a difference in this world and, consequently, I believed that I could deliver the services to make that vision a reality. I had belief in myself and my capabilities, and I knew that I was just a conduit for what the universe or God had in store for me.

Trust in the process
My life has turned out exactly the way it was meant to be. Everything about this process has afforded me an opportunity to actualize my mission. I had the column for over five years, producing two hundred sixty columns in all. Since my columns typically gave exercises and homework, I was able to create two different manuals to assist coaches and clients in "Carol the Coach" exercises for self-improvement and personal development.

My biggest dream is to run a ten-week series of Women's Empowerment Groups on *Oprah*, so I compiled a workbook for Ms. Winfrey, identifying the format. I am also doing a demo tape for XM and Sirius Radio, and was recently asked to submit three articles for *O* magazine. My radio shows highlighted other coaches and their niches, so I was able to spread the word about coaching and allow other coaches a forum to inspire and educate as well.

There are so many ways to coach others. I love the one-on-one, face-to-face work that I do on a daily basis. But what I have been called to do, involves reaching out to people through workshops, teleseminars, and through the media. This affords me the opportunity to globally reach out to many people to educate, motivate and inspire individual greatness. There are many other projects in the works, but each of them will come in its own time. I believe that God has many opportunities for me and, when I sit quietly and listen, I receive new ideas that are coming directly from Him to continue my mission. Spirituality, as you know, is a huge part of coaching. I live with the mantra that everything has it's time and that all the abundance in my life creates more abundance. If I do my part, the universe takes care of the rest.

There are no coincidences

As with coaching, I find that when you partner with the universe, you find some amazing things will happen, which may look like a coincidence. Let me share a story that happened to me, and you tell me what you think about the situation.

About halfway through my training, I decided that I needed to learn more about the law of attraction to increase my awareness of how I can work with the universe to effect change. I wanted to master some of the limiting beliefs that were imprinted, early in my life. I decided that I wanted to attract more abundance and prosperity in my life, which meant I needed to appreciate all the wonderful people, places and events that I had in my daily life. So, I told my colleagues at iPEC that I needed to study up on the law of attraction. They recommended eleven great books for me to read.

I immediately went to the library and started voraciously reading. Well, about ten days later, *The Secret* was released, and the whole world started talking about the law of attraction. I smiled to myself as I realized that I had attracted that "awareness" to my life. Now, I know that many of you might question whether that was merely a coincidence; however, I prefer to believe that I attracted exactly what I needed to my life. Coaching is a form of belief in oneself and in the world to co-create together.

Perhaps the hardest thing for me is to have patience, but, again, I default to iPEC's philosophy that the universe will arrange things for me if I get out of my own way. Besides that, it is the journey, not the destination, that really matters. So I continue to believe that lots of wonderful opportunities are in store for my client and me, if I trust the process and enjoy the ride!

Life as a River of Passion

JOURNEY

20

JAIME YORDAN-FRAU

Dreamer! This was a qualifier often associated with me as I was growing up—or, at least, so I thought. My parents and teachers did a fantastic job of pulling me down from the clouds and planting my feet firmly on the ground. Nonetheless, up until I was about thirty years old, my life could read as the account of a modern-day, life-purpose-seeking gypsy.

Where, when, and the circumstances of my birth—and possibly even my upbringing—may not be all that relevant for the sharing of this story and this part of my life. In school, like most of us, I had a few friends and many acquaintances, and I always felt liked by everyone. One thing I started noticing, though, yet did not give too much thought to, was the fact that people were drawn to me as a resource to help them solve all kinds of problems and issues...sometimes just to hear them out. Still, when it came time to choose a profession, to be inspired in the selection of what my life dedication would be, I chose to follow what most do—the expected.

In my years growing up, I wanted to be a doctor, a fireman, a policeman, a marine biologist, an actor, a performing-arts administrator (this one came later in life), etc. At times, the list seemed to be never-ending, providing a most comfortable sense of being good at many things and, possibly, of having a bright future. What I did not have was clarity, direction, focus and passion—a life purpose.

So, like a lot of people, I graduated high school and went straight to college. I decided to go for what seemed to be the most sensible option on my list and the one that my family seemed to be really good at; I went in as a pre-med major. I figured that I was good in sciences and interested by them, plus I liked helping people so...why not? Gratefully, during my first year, I took a required course in psychology and loved the philosophical and analytical nature of the discipline. That was the closest I had ever felt to being passionate about a field of interest— other than how much I loved acting—both in high school and college.

The problem with my passion for acting is that I never thought I was good enough and, once more, did not find the reinforcement to keep me focused on that career as a goal. Little did I know, this passion would later reemerge in my life, with a force that took me completely by surprise.

Going back to my story, I loved psychology; I really liked it a lot. So I did my very first taking-charge action and announced to my parents that I was changing majors, which I did. Interestingly, the area of psychology that I thought I would be most attracted to, clinical psychology, was completely obscured by the blessing of a professor whose chemistry with me was marginal, at best. I went through the program enjoying my education and being very participative in the department and its activities. I should also share that I got very good grades in the process and saw this as additional confirmation of being in the right direction.

When it came time to graduate from college, once more it felt like I was just riding the wave, moving with the flow, without a genuine focus or direction. As I sat listening—well not quite, but certainly thinking—to the guest speaker at the commencement ceremony, I remember thinking that I was going to pursue my master's degree in a field by which I was not enamored, yet, I couldn't think of anything better to do. In psychology, you could not just leave your academic preparation at a bachelor's-degree level, if you truly wanted to progress—so, off to my master's I went.

In my postgraduate studies, I had outstanding professors and a great study group and class. We received some praise and commendations due to our commitment and driven approach to our studies. You would never have guessed, but after graduating and starting to work in my chosen field, I ran away—far away—at the first chance of going after something that spoke to me, internally, something that made me feel more connected to myself, something I was passionate about. At the time, it was self-discovery, so I quit my job as an industrial-organizational consultant and went off to a forty-day, nonsectarian retreat in the mountains of New Mexico. It was an amazing experience, one that provided for much exploration and contemplation, yet little in finding out what my life's purpose was, what I was passionate about.

And then, life brought it to me—performing arts...once more. This time, the chosen form was dance and not acting. The force with which I fell in love with dancing, dance training and performing the difficult art of controlling your body in movement, made me forget anything and everything else as a career option.

For the following six years, I trained every day, and I danced every day, and the last four of the six years, I also became very involved in the administration of the performing-arts entities with which I became associated, both back home and in N.Y.C. Then, my early thirties hit, and my body started acting the way it should for someone who started in the profession as late as I did. Bottom line: life showed me the direction towards the next adventure, which was the corporate world.

At that time, I started a long and very prosperous career in that world. I began my adventure as a sales representative and, within eight years, I had achieved seven promotions—three vertical and four horizontal ones. I felt like I was flying, and I learned an unbelievable number of lessons that have allowed me—through coaching—to come back and discover what my true direction in life is. While on this wonderful ride, I felt that my inner needs for passion and purpose were being met by the sheer exhilaration of learning new tasks and responsibilities, pretty much every year-and-a-half. What seemed like my meteoric rise through the ranks, with top performance at every point in my career, even earned me the honor of serving the president of the company's U.S. operations as his chief-of-staff in matters pertaining to the field force.

Before I got to that position of honor and recognition, I had already started to analyze whether pursuing the continuation of that career path was what I truly wanted. Can you believe this? With so much success, I was questioning it all. Nonetheless, there was something that was not fulfilling to me. This is when I started to contemplate other possibilities, and I knew that being employed by another company would not fill the needs that I was discovering in my depths.

Interestingly, this awakening (as I call it) began when I became stationary in one position for the last four years of my career. At this point in my life I should have learned that, if there has been one constant in my life, it is that, if I allow it to, life pushes me and/or presents me with the next move, the next step, the next adventure.

This time around, life made it easy for me to move from where I was by putting, in my way, a colleague who—as the result of envy and his own incompetence—made it his mission to get me out of *his* way. Due to the recession that our nation had been going through at the time (another blessing?), I could not find another position within the company to move out my geography, and in doing so, save myself and my career from the Machiavellian reach of my colleague.

While all of this was happening, being quite vulnerable, as well as completely out in the open (my superior let it be known to me that what was going on with my colleague was justification for not granting me a promotion that had been well-earned), I continued to think about what I could do that I would be passionate about.

You see, at this point in my life, I had already learned that, in order to be completely happy and truly successful, one has to do what one is passionate about. My search took me to contemplate unimaginable options and then, one day, in talking with a friend, professional coaching was bought to the forefront of my search. Being very inquisitive, I continued to research the profession and decided that the most complete program—and best fit for me— was the iPEC coaching-certification program.

If I were to ask you, could you guess what happened in my life right after I discovered in which direction my life needed to go into? I believe you could.

One day, I find and decide that coaching was the right thing for me, and two weeks later I received the call…I was left without a job, after eleven years of stellar performance, in a company from which I thought I would retire at a very old age. But such is life. Now, I was offered a brand-new adventure—and what's most important, an adventure I could get passionate about.

I must tell you, when I first got into the coaching program, I did not know exactly what to expect. You know how some things sound one way on paper, and then when you experience them, they are not what you expected them to be? This certification program with iPEC coaching was no exception. In truth, I was not prepared to experience the energy that is felt during that first "Life's Potential" weekend, which is also considered the first of four face-to-face modules.

The depth of analysis that one undergoes as all the knowledge of the classes is shared, brought me to an almost contemplative state—and I say this because I had to force myself to remain alert and in the moment, in order to learn and benefit from all that was being shared. That first weekend module was, without a doubt, *the* cement that confirmed the correctness of my decision to become a professional coach.

Since that very first weekend, clarity of purpose and the discovery and realization of what I am truly passionate about in life, has continued to evolve, distilled and filtered, allowing me to achieve something I had only felt once before: true direction. For the first time in my life, I felt like I was in control of the direction my life was taking, instead of just going with the flow. Who would have thought that, under the circumstances where someone would feel least in control—losing one's job—I was on top of my self, my purpose and my direction in life, achieving ever more clarity on an almost daily basis. So far, this journey has brought many more discoveries about my life, about myself and about my reason for being. This journey has shown me that there is always something new to know, to discover, to learn, to grow from—to *live* for!

Through coaching, I have been able to balance my energy and center my life; acquire direction and focus while discovering my true purpose in life—that of helping and serving others. Coaching has taught me that life, in many ways, is like a river: it has a natural course and, although we may try to divert the river through building a new channel for it, when nature calls, the river seeks its natural course...this is the same with life, in general—this has been my biggest lesson.

We each come with a purpose, and we can discover and realize what that purpose is through the discovery of what makes us passionate in life. If we choose a different path from the one that this purpose meant for us to do with our lives, we tend to live extremely stressful and, mostly, unhappy lives—both states that we learn to live with, and even become desensitized to, as life goes on. To the fortunate ones, as I consider myself to be, even if the choice has not been in accordance with our natural or innate purpose, that river will pull them back to what they must do. Although this process is difficult and painful for a while, the fruit waiting to be plucked at the end of the redirection of one's life, is most sweet and extremely rewarding. All of this, I have learned so far, and I can only imagine all the wisdom yet to discover.

Now that I am here—and knowing that my purpose in life (among others) is to help people achieve happiness and success through discovering their purpose in life—I realize that I can only move forward if I can help bring this clarity and discovery to those who seek it. I want to ensure that I do all that I can to leave this world, at least, a little better than I found it. My way of doing that is in working with people and, through the process of coaching, help them achieve their highest potential in all aspects of their lives.

I intend to refocus the direction in which our educational system is currently moving our children—the future of the world—as they prepare to confront the challenges ahead. The reason I feel this way is that, right now, and by their own admission, educators' scope is too narrow: their focus is to ensure that our children succeed in school. Instead, this focus ought to be to ensure that our children succeed in *life*. It seems like a small change, but the shift in paradigms is huge—and the consequences could be of critical importance to our world, the future of society and humankind in general.

The engine that will allow this tremendous vision to come to life is the work that I will be doing through Integro Success Unlimited. Integro Success is my own coaching practice where our mission is to assist people in breaking free from what prevents them, their business and/or their careers from reaching full potential and greater levels of success. As our company name implies, integrity is at the core of who we are and how we choose to conduct ourselves.

Our company name also denotes our dedication to promoting *inter*nal *gro*wth—be it personal, professional or organizational—at all levels. At Integro Success, our coaching efforts are conducted in the most professional and confidential manner, where the focus is exclusively on our clients and their goals. Through exploration, discovery, analysis and accountability, we deliver on our commitment to assist clients in moving forward and reaching their goals.

At this moment, we stand at the verge of great things, all of them tied to our central passion. As a summation of the latest up-

"...we stand at the verge of great things, all of them tied to our central passion"

dates in the life of Integro Success Unlimited, we have officially finished our website (www.integrosuccess.com) and would like to invite you to come in and explore our services and scope. We have also been working closely with local colleges, universities and private/charter high schools in exploring the applicability of our concept into their curriculum or, at least, as an additional resource for parents to explore in giving their children the best opportunities to succeed in life. We have also been approached by a local TV station interested in doing a news segment on us and what we are doing to increase people's chances at reaching higher levels of success in life.

Although there are many more smaller milestones that have been achieved, I will close this summary by sharing that Integro Success, through our proprietary program The Passionate Future Project, sees our services as the best thing we can do to give back to our community and society in general. For this reason, we will continue exploring any and every avenue that will allow us to help as many people as possible to increase their chances at a highly successful life through the discovery of their true passions and the development of a plan to create their most successful life out of that passion.

Why don't you join us in making the world a better place by discovering what your passions are and how they can be turned into an extremely rewarding, joyous and successful life?

Awaken your passion—achieve your success. Contact us at info@integrosuccess.com, and let's start your journey.

BUSINESS PROFILES

Where Are
the Coaches
Now in
Their Journeys?

ABEL Business Institute

Ed Abel

ABEL Business Institute was founded to provide business owners with strategies, support, education, and guidance throughout the stages of their business development. Through years of hands-on business experience, we have developed a systematic approach to the construction, growth, and maintenance of businesses; this approach is our methodology.

We have a passion for business development and we empathize with those who feel challenged, confused and unsure about the approach to their business. Our objective is to assist business owners through the process of establishing an effective plan, understand the methodology and implement an action plan to foster the growth and progression of their business.

Through extensive and objective analysis, we identify obstacles and set priorities by designing a plan of action that capitalizes on the strengths of your company and supports your weaknesses. In addition, we teach and implement various business tools that utilize principles and systems that we have created and mastered during our 25 years of business development.

Judi Rhee Alloway

In the Asian-American community, Judi Rhee Alloway serves as National Chairwoman of Women in National Association of Asian American Professionals (WIN), a diversity leadership-training program launched in 2009, cultivating the Asian-American leaders of tomorrow. We have a network of members spanning over 20 chapters and 14 ventures of NAAAP in metropolitan cities across the United States and Canada. Research us at http://www.naaap.org. Also locally recognized as a community leader, she is also a 2010 Pennsylvania Political Fellows for the Center of Progressive Leadership. Find more information at http://www.progressiveleaders.org.

In the multicultural health and wellness field, Judi Rhee Alloway is the co-founder of REAL Raw Life, a local support and transformation group plus global online community that supports people in becoming and remaining raw vegans/live foodists. Check us out at http://www.realrawlife.com.

Please feel free to contact me at judi.rhee.alloway@gmail.com and 856.952.2269 if you have any questions about the coach training program and my budding coaching practice.

Seed Word Communications, LLC
P.O. Box 16615, Tallahassee, FL 32317
www.seedword.com
Office phone: +1.850.765.0386
Mobile phone: +1.850.321.7620

Dr. Joseph Amanfu,
PMP, CCP, MBCS, CTM, CPC, ELI-MP, Ph.D.
Leadership Coach
joe.amanfu@seedword.com

Through leadership coaching, let us help you develop your
- *Motivation:* What can move us toward adjusting, changing, and growing?
- *Effectiveness:* What can I do to develop my true potential?
- *Leadership:* How can I become the leader I want to be and develop productive leadership skills?

  We want to help you find the motivation and develop the skills to become an effective leader and maximize your full potential. For many years, it has been my privilege to work with people across the world within many different settings. It is my hope that I can help you make the adjustments you need in your life and realize the goals you have in business, in relationships, and in life.

"The pessimist complains about the wind. The optimist expects it to change. The leader adjusts the sails."
—John Maxwell, *The 21 Irrefutable Laws of Leadership*

The W.A.Y. Coaching, Inc.
www.theweddingaccordingtoyou.com
630-231-0600

Raechel Anderson Dressler,
MBA, CPC, ACC, ELI-MP
President and Founder
raechel@theweddingaccordingtoyou.com

It is safe to say that brides who are planning a wedding typically feel a lot of stress and relationship strain and often struggle to have the wedding they truly want. Raechel is a bridal coach and the creator of the innovative Wedding According to You coaching system, which champions brides to have a fabulous wedding experience by partnering with them to learn and implement new skills, concepts and habits that reduce stress and relationship strain, and empower brides to create the wedding they truly want...*and* a lifetime of sustainable, successful personal growth. Raechel believes every bride can have the wedding of her dreams, regardless of her circumstances.

Raechel is the founder of The W.A.Y. Coaching. Her passion for coaching stems out of passions that Raechel has: big-picture and perspective mastery, empathy and understanding for those struggling to find happiness and joy in their lives, and moving forward "regardless."

When you're ready to create a Wedding According to You, Raechel is the one to turn to!

Appelbaum Wellness LLC
www.appelbaumwellness.com
847.236.1330

**Barbara B. Appelbaum,
CPC, ELI-MP, MBA, MAT**
info@appelbaumwellness.com

Entering the second half of one's life and experiencing the aging process can be the most exciting time, and the most stressful. Worries of
transitioning from what "was" to what "will be"
can be overwhelming. Fears of illness, identifying oneself by one's former life roles (parent, executive, etc.) cloud your mind. If you are anything like other people
who are coming face-to-face with their aging process, you know that
time is precious and you want to find fulfillment, a sense of purpose
as well as joy.

You might have lost that sense of balance: the mind-body-spirit
connection. Your feelings of confusion, dissatisfaction and boredom
are understandable and quite normal. How would it feel if you could
take control of your life, health and wellness and create an abundant
life?

We offer individual and small-business coaching, assessments and
workshops geared toward those facing these challenges. Please visit
our website to begin your personal wellness journey and learn to
"Live in Wellness Now™."

get inspired. get in the game.

Jennifer Barley, PCC, CPC
www.jenniferbarley.com
jennifer@jenniferbarley.com
831.212.2793

Jennifer Barley is a certified professional life coach, public speaker, lead trainer for the Institute for Professional Excellence in Coaching (iPEC), author and former award-winning Weight Watchers leader.

As your health and wellness coach, Jennifer specializes in learning how your insides affect your outside when it comes to food and exercise choices. She has the ability to help you understand how your thoughts drive your feelings which drive your actions. As your partner, Jennifer helps you tap into your greatest potential to create whatever life you choose.

Stephanie Davis Life Coaching
www.stephaniedavislifecoaching.com

Stephanie Davis

13.1 miles later, Stephanie finishes her second half-marathon; tired, thrilled, and happy to have coached herself through another one.

Stephanie Davis is an inspirational speaker, writer, and professional life coach. Stephanie has empowered and motivated her youngest daughter to find happiness and success while battling a rare degenerative brain disease and partial paralysis. Helping her daughter learn to sit, stand, and walk a second time around has created a very meaningful appreciation of health, humor, and leadership, which are integrated throughout her coaching programs and workshops.

Stephanie is a certified professional coach, a proud volunteer for the Epilepsy Foundation of Florida and leads the nonprofit organization The Olivia Davis Foundation, dedicated to helping families of catastrophic epilepsy and other chronic health conditions.

A+ Life Development
www.apluslifedevelopment.com

Tim Durling
tim@apluslifedevelopment.com.

A+ Life Development is dedicated to helping functional people become optimal in order to realize their goals and dreams. By using the latest in healthy, positive, and enabling coaching and hypnotherapy techniques, we help people to thrive personally and professionally. Through our processes, clients deepen their learning, improve their performance, and enhance their quality of life.

After a successful 25-year career working with information systems in corporate America, founder Tim Durling decided to give back to society on a personal level by dedicating the second half of his adult work life to the field of life coaching. While enrolled in training at the Institute for Professional Excellence in Coaching, he realized that the power of the subconscious mind can safely and effectively be accessed through hypnotherapy. The combination of coaching and hypnotherapy has proved a strong venue for helping clients rid themselves of habits, hangups, and hurts that no longer serve them well, while simultaneously developing new positive skills and attitudes to thrust them into the promising future of their choice.

In addition, Tim is an entrepreneur, a student of higher consciousness and theology, and the proud father of two beautiful daughters. A resident of the Greater Tampa Bay area in Florida, he is a member of the Tampa Bay Professional Coaches Association, the International Coaching Federation, and the International Association of Counselors and Therapists.

Powerful Purpose Associates
www.powerfulpurpose.com

Anthony Fasano

At Powerful Purpose Associates, we use the coaching process to help our clients maximize their potential in all aspects of their business as well as their personal development. We do this by forming an alliance with our clients to help them move forward to quickly and effectively achieve their goals, creating success!

Our company name is based on our belief that there is a powerful purpose in coaching in that it prompts client-generated strategies and solutions. Coaching stretches people to do things that they never thought they could do.

Our Career-Biz Booster Program was designed specifically to help people develop and expand their careers and businesses. The program helps you focus on and develop six key business components that will help you become a huge success in your field.

Visit our website at www.powerulpurpose.com and sign up for our free *Monday Morning Motivator*. Start to bring some inspiration into your life on a weekly basis! It's one of the many ways we help people reach their potential!

Just Traders International, LLC
JTI Coaching
P.O. Box 244
Glendale Maryland, MD 20720
www.tinafrizzell.com
Office Phone: +1.301.249.6077
Mobile Phone: +1.301.704.8181

Tina Frizzell-Jenkins, CPC
ELI Master Practitioner
Home-Based Business & Tax-Savings Coach
Empowerment Coach
Leadership Coach
tina@tinafrizzell.com

Just Traders International, LLC is your professional and courteous service company. We provide quality business, transportation and e-commerce service. We operate out of the Washington, DC, metropolitan area, but we do business internationally as well. We believe customer service is not a department, but an attitude.

Coach with Tina, the home-based business-empowerment coach, seminar speaker/trainer and tax advisor. Tina is responsible for empowering hundreds of people just like you to keep the money they earn with her proven system of wealth-building techniques!

What do you enjoy? Partner with Tina and JTI coaching to pursue taking your purpose to profit!

Mastery Associates
www.masteryassociates.com
516.835.8027

Ronit Hakimi
CPC, ELI Master Practitioner
Founder and CEO
ronit@masteryassociates.com

At Mastery Associates, we are passionately committed to our client's commitment. We intently listen and partner with our clients to identify, implement, and attain extraordinary results. Our mission is to excel in empowering our clients to create a life of happiness, purpose and fulfillment; to create a life journey filled with awareness, choices, light and love.

We develop and implement character- and value-education programs for elementary schools. Entertaining, fun, engaging, transformational programs that educate and inspire! Through hands-on activities, games, role-playing and book-reading, the children are able to tap into the power and divinity within themselves and achieve greater self-confidence, connection, responsibility, teamwork and cooperation. Our purpose is to assist schools, teachers and administrators to develop a solid positive foundation for life-long learning.

We also offer excellence in coaching to families, groups, corporations and individuals who are committed to obtaining mastery in life. Using energy and transformational techniques, we are able to move our clients into sustainable extraordinary results; results which are aligned with the clients values, goals and purpose.

Please visit our website and contact us with any questions, comments and/or insights.

Soaring Solutions
Empowering the Flight **of Your Life.**

Soaring Solutions
www.soaringsolutions.net

Sue Koch

Sue Koch has learned the exceptional power of the coaching process and discovered a new passion for a career path, founding Chicago-based Soaring Solutions, LLC. Working with individuals and businesses to inspire and motivate change, we help them build a solid foundation for continued growth and success.

Sue Koch spent 15 years in consulting and corporate roles, building and managing the internal business systems and organizational structures of small technology companies in Chicago. Joining companies in new or growth phases gave her exceptional coverage in all aspects of running a business. This provided keen insight into what it takes to succeed in both the short and long term, and what needs to be in place to sustain a growing business and retain productive, happy employees.

Her management experience and style have proven very effective in mentoring staff, mediating conflict, and ensuring that people are given the opportunity to grow and thrive as they deserve. Her training as a professional business and life coach at the Institute for Professional Excellence in Coaching provides the formal training, structure and toolset to support what Sue has been offering employees and peers for many years. The result of a positive environment and thriving happy employees is a successful business.

In addition, Sue's personal experience in career transition, personal traumas and heavy focus on performance fitness and injury recovery position her well to coach others, with compassion and understanding, through similar experiences and guide them to achieve their goals with great success and motivation.

Kilian Kröll
www.kiliankroell.com
facebook.com/kiliankroell
coach@kiliankroell.com
kiliankroell@gmail.com
215.717.8424

Perhaps you want to experience full creative freedom inside the institution that funds you. Maybe you consider yourself an agent of change who feels held back by a world that doesn't get you. Sometimes, providing for your basic needs gets in the way of experiencing true passion for life. Other times, you get itchy feet and abandon projects, people and places in the search for your inner self.

Kilian Kröll is a global nomad, modern dancer, cultural scholar and certified Core Energy Coach™. He empowers right-brain creative and intellectual people to thrive amongst the hierarchical, left-brain institutional structures that support their work. He provides teachers and artists with the tools to deeply connect with their students and audiences. Kilian's mission is to help his clients shift their perspectives, motivations and actions so they become fully at home in every world they inhabit.

 IngeniousYou

IngeniousYou

Samita Loomba
Executive and Leadership Coach
www.ingeniousyou.com

Are you wondering about the name of my business, "IngeniousYou?" I believe that all human beings are smart, intelligent, gifted, bright and capable of tapping into their inner genius and creating a life of their dreams.

Executive and Leadership Coaching takes you through a "Leadership Empowerment Program." The program relates to the concept of leadership skills and gives you a chance to realize how you may use your leadership in all aspects of your life, and not just the professional aspect. The program will give you an opportunity to work through the challenges that you might be facing or simply strengthen the skills you may already have.

The concept is not to make something out of you that is not *you* but to empower you with the tools that you can use to align your outer and inner self to create a life of your own truth. I can imagine you telling yourself, "Oh, this is not for me, because I am not an executive or a leader." I challenge you to ask yourself the question, "Who is leading my life?"

You are the leader of your own life. You are the CEO, CIO, CTO, marketing director, finance firector, entertainment director and general staff of your life. You go through all these roles every day of your life. Now that we have clarified the leadership concept, ask yourself; "How do I want to lead my life and make it what I really dream for it to be?"

IngeniousYou will partner with you in helping you on your journey to a very healthy, happy, productive and fulfilling life.

C3—Culturally Creative Coaching

Kari Lowrey Sadler

C3 is a professional coaching and facilitation company that was designed with culturally creative people in mind. Specializing in time management, juggling multiple roles, and taking care of yourself, we are dedicated to providing the highest quality of facilitation, professional coaching and public speaking.

Want to learn more about where your energy is going? Check out the *NEW* Energy Leadership™ Assessment.

Kari Lowrey Saddler is the owner of C3. She has her MBA, ACC, ELI-MP is a certified professional coach, a member of the International Coach Federation, a member of the Tampa Bay Professional Coach Association, a lead trainer for the Institute for Professional Excellence in Coaching, a lead trainer for Book Yourself Solid, and a member of the Tampa Bay Area Professional Speakers' Association. She is also a wife and mother.

Phoenix Consulting Alliance

Julie McManus
julie@phoenixconsultingalliance.com
Blog: www.juliemcmanuscoach.wordpress.com
937.210.0409

Phoenix Consulting Alliance is a group of impassioned professionals who work with organizations to improve their employee engagement and customer service.

Those organizations with engaged employees have been proven to have greater customer retention, greater return on assets, reduced employee turnover, reduced hiring and retention costs, improved productivity, and more financially sound results.

Engagement is about establishing trust, employee recognition, encouraging autonomy, creating opportunities, aligning goals and creating passion. Passion for the organization and passion for the customer.

Those organizations that have created an engaged workforce have reaped huge benefits as a result. They stand above their competitors and are showcased as the ones to beat.

Are you engaged? Are your employees engaged? If not, let us help you.

Phoenix Consulting Alliance uses a combination of coaching and consulting practices to create a successful partnership. We deliver the results you desire and work with you to ensure your satisfaction. Projects will typically include assessments, workshops, training and various interventions based on need.

REDDYWORKS
New Tools for Vibrant Growth

ReddyWorks
www.reddyworks.com

Michael Reddy

We work both with individuals, and a variety of wellness and education providers. Motivated clients typically achieve seriously improved levels of health, functionality, and fulfillment—either for themselves, or their own clients, or both. We help them transform challenges like chronic disease, deeply embedded family conflicts, change-resistant patterns of failure, and business instability (either too much or too little)—into opportunities for growth, harmony, and greater abundance.

Coaching and Constellations—Our unique combination of transformational coaching and systemic constellation work resolves problems that prove difficult for narrower approaches. Constellations reveal and re-align misplaced loyalties within families or small businesses both effectively and inexpensively. These remain otherwise very often hidden. In that state, they can undermine growth and wellness in ways that make pure coaching, therapy, and treatments for chronic conditions ineffective.

Coaching in our work leads thus sometimes to constellations that release group-level blockages when they stand in the way. In the other direction, constellation clients attain both new insight and a deep shift in inner, felt awareness. At times this is sufficient. But experienced, perceptive coaching helps some to ground and implement external changes enabled by the shift.

Energy Leadership Assessments—Less than half-an-hour of online responses provides a comprehensive picture of how clients use seven different types of energy as they engage with life. This assessment is dynamic, can be taken again, and reflects changes as they learn and grow. iPEC's research and our experience show that shifting their use of these energies in easily understood directions significantly increases their satisfaction in life and business. We recommend and work with this, as well as standard 360-degree assessments.

Marketing and Operations—We are licensed to train interested clients in Michael Port's bestselling "Book Yourself Solid" approach to marketing professional practices and small service businesses. This is a strategic, "best of its kind" system based on core passion, integrity, and the delivery of value and genuine love to all contacts. It really works, even for those who have disliked marketing and networking. Beyond this, decades of experience in structuring technology and operations for a range of businesses position us to help organize people and machines to handle the growth our clients create.

Rodas Coaching, LLC

Deborah Sakelaris
Professional Certified Life Coach, Energy
   Leadership Master Practitioner
deborah@rodascoaching.com
312.798.7404

Deborah is a certified professional coach, Master Energy Leadership practitioner and a professional public speaker. She is also the owner of Rodas Coaching, LLC, a company dedicated to helping individuals create passion, joy and success in their lives. Deborah's coaching expertise is in life transitions, work/life balance and Energy Leadership.

Deborah is trained by the Coaches Training Institute and iPEC, both fully accredited internationally recognized coaching programs.

With a bachelor's degree in journalism/PR and a master's degree in business from Ball State University, Deborah has over 15 years of progressive experience in training and development with expertise in the areas of coaching, operational management, recruiting, and program development. In addition, Deborah has managed, trained and coached 47 franchise owners and their staffs in all areas of the employment industry.

She is an active member of professional and volunteer organizations including the International Coaches Federation, the National Association of Women Business Owners, the Professional Women's Club of Chicago, and the Catholic Charities Organization. She is also on the board of Get Healthy Chicago.

Carol the Coach Services
Personal Life Coaching
www.carolthecoach.com

Carol Juergensen Sheets

Carol has committed herself to helping you achieve your goals. Not only is she a trained psychotherapist, but she recently obtained her certification from the Institute for Personal Excellence in Coaching. Carol is Indianapolis's most recognizable coach and has helped thousands with her life skills on television, on her own radio show and in magazines and newspapers.

Carol is ready to speak with you by phone or in person to assist you in creating the life you deserve.

Let Carol assist you in breaking free of your fears and limiting beliefs so that you can finally accomplish your dreams!

Isn't it time you developed the action plan that will move you forward in mastering your goals?

Are you ready to create extraordinary results that improve your productivity, your relationships and your self-esteem?

Work with Carol for one to three months and watch the changes occur! Email her now for the special promotional offer that will save you money while you develop the strategies to make your life happen.

Integro Success Unlimited
www.integrosuccess.com

Jaime Yordan-Frau

Like the dragon in our logo that breaks free from the sphere that holds it back, our mission is to assist you in breaking free from what holds you, your business or your career back from reaching full potential and greater levels of success.

As our company name implies, integrity is at the core of who we are and how we choose to conduct ourselves. Our company name also denotes our dedication to promoting *Inte*rnal *Gro*wth—be it personal, professional or organizational—at all levels.

At Integro, our coaching efforts are conducted in the most professional and confidential manner, where the focus is exclusively on you and your goals. Through exploration, discovery, analysis and accountability we deliver on our commitment to assist you in moving forward and reaching your goals.

If there was ever a time when it was critically important to be on top of your continued success, it is now—today. Call us and explore the possibilities!

Prescott Design
prescottdesignshop.com

Alan Prescott
Graphic design/copywriting/web presence
prescott_alan@comcast.net
949.412.4548

Hired in 1975 as a foot messenger for a small typesetting business in New York City, Alan founded his own business six years later and transformed it into one of the most profitable boutique typeshops in Manhattan. After the successful completion of over 30,000 projects, he went on to found Prescott Design in the '90s with the slogan "Affordable graphic design from our small business to yours."

Alan's background in typography and an extensive interest in photography, art history and language have enabled him to bring unique and durable perspectives on the marriage of words to images, creating for his clients an extraordinarily powerful way to rise above the clutter in today's saturated markets.

The value in your business is already there because you believe in it, but bringing that richness to the consumer can be frustrating if you do it alone and often too expensive when you bring it to the Big Guys. Putting Prescott Design on your team means you can do what you do best: building relationships, creating value in your products and services, and opening up new vistas on your amazing journeys.

International Coach Federation

The International Coach Federation (ICF)

The information below is copyrighted by the International Coach Federation (ICF) and reprinted with permission (Source: www.coach federation.org). Please be encouraged to visit the ICF website for additional information.

Founded in 1995, the International Coach Federation (ICF) is the leading global organization dedicated to advancing the coaching profession by setting high standards, providing independent certification, and building a worldwide network of credentialed coaches.

With more than 13,000 professional, personal and business coaches, representing over 90 countries, the ICF is the voice of the global coaching profession.

ICF Core Purpose: *To advance the art, science and practice of professional coaching.*

What is Coaching?

The ICF defines coaching as partnering with clients in a thought-provoking and creative process that inspires them to maximize their personal and professional potential.

Coaching honors the client as the expert in his/her life and work and believes that every client is creative, resourceful, and whole.

Standing on this foundation, the coach's responsibility is to:

Discover, clarify, and align with what the client wants to achieve;

Encourage client self-discovery;

Elicit client-generated solutions and strategies; and

Hold the client responsible and accountable.

Professional coaches provide an ongoing partnership designed to help clients produce fulfilling results in their personal and professional lives. Coaches help people improve their performances and enhance the quality of their lives.

Coaches are trained to listen, to observe and to customize their approach to individual client needs. They seek to elicit solutions and strategies from the client; they believe the client is naturally creative and resourceful. The coach's job is to provide support to enhance the skills, resources, and creativity that the client already has.

How can you determine if coaching is right for you?

To determine if you could benefit from coaching, start by summarizing what you would expect to accomplish in coaching. When someone has a fairly clear idea of the desired outcome, a coaching partnership can be a useful tool for developing a strategy for how to achieve that outcome with greater ease.

Since coaching is a partnership, also ask yourself if you find it valuable to collaborate, to have another viewpoint and to be asked to consider new perspectives. Also, ask yourself if you are ready to devote the time and the energy to making real changes in your work or life. If the answer to these questions is yes, then coaching may be a beneficial way for you to grow and develop.

How is coaching distinct from other service professions?

Professional coaching is a distinct service which focuses on an individual's life as it relates to goal setting, outcome creation and personal change management. In an effort to understand what a coach is, it can be helpful to distinguish coaching from other professions that provide personal or organizational support.

Therapy: Coaching can be distinguished from therapy in a number of ways. First, coaching is a profession that supports personal and professional growth and development based on individual-initiated change in pursuit of specific actionable outcomes. These outcomes are linked to personal or professional success.

Coaching is forward moving and future focused. Therapy, on the other hand, deals with healing pain, dysfunction and conflict within an individual or a relationship between two or more individuals. The focus is often on resolving difficulties arising from the past which hamper an individual's emotional functioning in the present, improving overall psychological functioning, and dealing with present life and work circumstances in more emotionally healthy ways. Therapy outcomes often include improved emotional/feeling states. While positive feelings/emotions may be a natural outcome of coaching, the primary focus is on creating actionable strategies for achieving specific goals in one's work or personal life. The emphasis in a coaching relationship is on action, accountability and follow through.

Consulting: Consultants may be retained by individuals or organizations for the purpose of accessing specialized expertise. While consulting approaches vary widely, there is often an assumption that the consultant diagnoses problems and prescribes and sometimes implements solutions. In general, the assumption with coaching is that individuals or teams are capable of generating their own solutions, with the coach supplying supportive, discovery-based approaches and frameworks.

Mentoring: Mentoring, which can be thought of as guiding from one's own experience or sharing of experience in a specific area of industry or career development, is sometimes confused with coaching. Although some coaches provide mentoring as part of their coaching, such as in mentor coaching new coaches, coaches are not typically mentors to those they coach.

Training: Training programs are based on the acquisition of certain learning objectives as set out by the trainer or instructor. Though objectives are clarified in the coaching process, they are set by the individual or team being coached with guidance provided by the coach. Training also assumes a linear learning path which coincides with an established curriculum. Coaching is less linear without a set curriculum plan.

Athletic Development: Though sports metaphors are often used, professional coaching is different from the traditional sports coach. The athletic coach is often seen as an expert who guides and directs the behavior of individuals or teams based on his or her greater experience and knowledge. Professional coaches possess these qualities, but it is the experience and knowledge of the individual or team that determines the direction. Additionally, professional coaching, unlike athletic development, does not focus on behaviors that are being executed poorly or incorrectly. Instead, the focus is on identifying opportunity for development based on individual strengths and capabilities.

What are some typical reasons someone might work with a coach?

There are many reasons that an individual or team might choose to work with a coach, including but not limited to the following:

> There is something at stake (a challenge, stretch goal or opportunity), and it is urgent, compelling or exciting or all of the above;

> There is a gap in knowledge, skills, confidence, or resources;

> There is a desire to accelerate results;

> There is a lack of clarity, and there are choices to be made;

> The individual is extremely successful, and success has started to become problematic;

> Work and life are out of balance, and this is creating unwanted consequences; or

> One has not identified his or her core strengths and how best to leverage them.

What has caused the tremendous growth in the coaching industry?

Coaching has grown significantly for many reasons. Generally the world has changed a lot, and coaching is a useful tool to deal with many of those changes. For example, coaching is a great tool for today's challenging job market. There is more job transition, more self-employment and small business. Some of the real life factors include:

Rapid changes in the external business environment;

Downsizing, restructuring, mergers and other organizational changes have radically altered what has been termed the "traditional employment contract"-companies can no longer achieve results using traditional management approaches;

There is a growing shortage of talented employees in certain industries-to attract and retain top talent, companies must commit to investing in individuals' development;

There is a widening disparity between what managers were trained to do and what their jobs now require them to do in order to meet increasing demands for competitive results;

There is unrest on the part of many employees and leaders in many companies-people are wrestling with fears around job insecurity and increased workplace pressures to perform at higher levels than ever before;

Companies must develop inclusive, collaborative work environments, in order to achieve strategic business goals, and to maintain high levels of customer satisfaction; and

Individuals who have experienced the excellent results of coaching are talking to more people about coaching. In short, coaching helps people focus on what matters most to them in life: business and personal. People today are more open to the idea of being in charge of their own lives. Coaching helps people do just that; so the industry continues to grow.

How is coaching delivered? What does the process look like?
The Coaching Process: Coaching typically begins with a personal interview (either face-to-face or by teleconference call) to as-

sess the individual's current opportunities and challenges, define the scope of the relationship, identify priorities for action, and establish specific desired outcomes. Subsequent coaching sessions may be conducted in person or over the telephone, with each session lasting a previously established length of time. Between scheduled coaching sessions, the individual may be asked to complete specific actions that support the achievement of one's personally prioritized goals. The coach may provide additional resources in the form of relevant articles, checklists, assessments, or models, to support the individual's thinking and actions. The duration of the coaching relationship varies depending on the individual's personal needs and preferences.

Assessments: A variety of assessments are available to support the coaching process, depending upon the needs and circumstances of the individual. Assessments provide objective information which can enhance the individual's self-awareness as well as awareness of others and their circumstances, provide a benchmark for creating coaching goals and actionable strategies, and offer a method for evaluating progress.

Concepts, models and principles: A variety of concepts, models and principles drawn from the behavioral sciences, management literature, spiritual traditions and/or the arts and humanities, may be incorporated into the coaching conversation in order to increase the individual's self-awareness and awareness of others, foster shifts in perspective, promote fresh insights, provide new frameworks for looking at opportunities and challenges, and energize and inspire the individual's forward actions.

Appreciative approach: Coaching incorporates an appreciative approach. The appreciative approach is grounded in what's right, what's working, what's wanted, and what's needed to get there. Using an appreciative approach, the coach models constructive communication skills and methods the individual or team can utilize to enhance personal communication effectiveness. The appreciative approach incorporates discovery-based inquiry, proactive (as opposed to reactive) ways of managing personal opportunities and challenges, constructive framing of observations and feedback in order to elicit the most positive responses from others, and envisioning success as contrasted with focusing on problems. The appreciative approach is simple to understand and employ, but its effects in harnessing possibility thinking and goal-oriented action can be profound.

How long does a coach work with an individual?

The length of a coaching partnership varies depending on the individual's or team's needs and preferences. For certain types of focused coaching, 3 to 6 months of working with a coach may work. For other types of coaching, people may find it beneficial to work with a coach for a longer period. Factors that may impact the length of time include: the types of goals, the ways individuals or teams like to work, the frequency of coaching meetings, and financial resources available to support coaching.

How do you ensure a compatible partnership?

Overall, be prepared to design the coaching partnership with the coach. For example, think of a strong partnership that you currently have in your work or life. Look at how you built that relationship and what is important to you about partnership. You will want to build those same things into a coaching relationship. Here are a few other tips:

> Have a personal interview with one or more coaches to determine "what feels right" in terms of the chemistry. Coaches are accustomed to being interviewed, and there is generally no charge for an introductory conversation of this type.

> Look for stylistic similarities and differences between the coach and you and how these might support your growth as an individual or the growth of your team.

> Discuss your goals for coaching within the context of the coach's specialty or the coach's preferred way of working with a individual or team

> Talk with the coach about what to do if you ever feel things are not going well; make some agreements up front on how to handle questions or problems.

> Remember that coaching is a partnership, so be as-

sertive about talking with the coach about anything that is of concern at any time.

Within the partnership, what does the coach do? The individual?

The role of the coach is to provide objective assessment and observations that foster the individual's or team members' enhanced self-awareness and awareness of others, practice astute listening in order to garner a full understanding of the individual's or team's circumstances, be a sounding board in support of possibility thinking and thoughtful planning and decision making, champion opportunities and potential, encourage stretch and challenge commensurate with personal strengths and aspirations, foster the shifts in thinking that reveal fresh perspectives, challenge blind spots in order to illuminate new possibilities, and support the creation of alternative scenarios. Finally, the coach maintains professional boundaries in the coaching relationship, including confidentiality, and adheres to the coaching profession's code of ethics.

The role of the individual or team is to create the coaching agenda based on personally meaningful coaching goals, utilize assessment and observations to enhance self-awareness and awareness of others, envision personal and/or organizational success, assume full responsibility for personal decisions and actions, utilize the coaching process to promote possibility thinking and fresh perspectives, take courageous action in alignment with personal goals and aspirations, engage big picture thinking and problem solving skills, and utilize the tools, concepts, models and principles provided by the coach to engage effective forward actions.

What does coaching ask of an individual?

To be successful, coaching asks certain things of the individual, all of which begin with intention. Additionally, clients should:

Focus—on one's self, the tough questions, the hard truths—and one's success.

Observe—the behaviors and communications of others.

Listening—to one's intuition, assumptions, judgments, and to the way one sounds when one speaks.

Self discipline—to challenge existing attitudes, beliefs and behaviors and to develop new ones which serve one's goals in a superior way.

Style—leveraging personal strengths and overcoming limitations in order to develop a winning style.

Decisive actions—however uncomfortable, and in spite of personal insecurities, in order to reach for the exraordinary.

Compassion—for one's self as he or she experiments with new behaviors, experiences setbacks-and for others as they do the same.

Humor—committing to not take one's self so seriously, using humor to lighten and brighten any situation.

Personal control—maintaining composure in the face of disappointment and unmet expectations, avoiding emotional reactivity.

Courage—to reach for more than before, to shift out of being fear based in to being in abundance as a core strategy for success, to engage in continual self examination, to overcome internal and external obstacles.

How can the success of the coaching process be measured?
Measurement may be thought of in two distinct ways. First, there are the external indicators of performance: measures which can be seen and measured in the individual's or team's environment. Second, there are internal indicators of success: measures which are inherent within the individual or team members being coached and can be measured by the individual or team being coached with the support of the coach. Ideally, both external and internal metrics are incorporated.

Examples of external measures include achievement of coaching goals established at the outset of the coaching relationship, increased income/revenue, obtaining a promotion, performance feedback which is obtained from a sample of the individual's constituents (e.g., direct reports, colleagues, customers, boss, the manager him/herself), personal and/or business performance data (e.g., productivity, efficiency measures). The external measures selected should ideally be things the individual is already measuring and are things the individual has some ability to directly influence.

Examples of internal measures include self-scoring/self-validating assessments that can be administered initially and at regular intervals in the coaching process, changes in the individual's self-awareness and awareness of others, shifts in thinking which inform more effective actions, and shifts in one's emotional state which inspire confidence.

What are the factors that should be considered when looking at the financial investment in coaching?

Working with a coach requires both a personal commitment of time and energy as well as a financial commitment. Fees charged vary by specialty and by the level of experience of the coach. Individuals should consider both the desired benefits as well as the anticipated length of time to be spent in coaching. Since the coaching relationship is predicated on clear communication, any financial concerns or questions should be voiced in initial conversations before the agreement is made. The ICF Coach Referral Service allows you to search for a coach based on a number of qualifications including fee range.

Further Reading

The following is a list of the resources and/or authors mentioned in this book:

Bandler, R., Grinder, J. *Frogs into Princes: Neuro Linguistic Programming*. Boulder, CO: Real People Press, 1979.

Bernd, Jr., Ed. *Jose Silva's Ultramind ESP System: Think Your Way to Success*. Franklin Lakes, NJ: Career Press, 2000.

Berg, I.K. *Family Based Services: A Solution-Focused Approach*. New York: Norton. 1994.

Cohen, Dan Booth. *I Carry Your Heart in My Heart: Family Constellations in Prison*. Heidelberg: Carl Auer International, 2009.

Csikszentmihályi, Mihaly. *Beyond Boredom and Anxiety: Experiencing Flow in Work and Play*. San Francisco: Jossey-Bass, 1975.

Csikszentmihályi, Mihaly. *Flow: The Psychology of Optimal Experience*. New York: Harper Perennial Modern Classics, 2008.

Erickson, Milton H., Rossi, Ernest L. *Hypnotherapy: An Exploratory Casebook*. New York: Irvington Publishers, 1979.

Fenwick, Sheridan. *Getting It: The Psychology of est*. Philadelphia,: J.B. Lippincott, 1976.

Hill, Napoleon. *Think and Grow Rich*. New York: Random House Publishing Group, 1987.

Leonard, Thomas. *The 28 Laws of Attraction: Stop Chasing Success and Let It Chase You*. New York: Scribner, 2007.

Patterson, Kerry et al. *Crucial Conversations: Tools for Talking When Stakes Are High*. New York: McGraw-Hill, 2002.

Payne, John L. *The Healing of Individuals, Families & Nations: Transgenerational Healing & Family Constellations*. Findhorn, Scot.: Findhorn Press, 2005.

Peale, Norman Vincent. *The Power of Positive Thinking*. New York: Simon & Schuster, 2009.

Port, Michael. *Book Yourself Solid*. New York: John Wiley & Sons, Inc., 2006.

Port, Michael, Marshall, Elizabeth. *The Contrarian Effect: Why It Pays (Big) to Take Typical Sales Advice and Do the Opposite*. New York: John Wiley & Sons, Inc., 2008.

Port, Michael, Samuels, Mina. *The Think Big Manifesto: Think You Can't Change Your Life (and the World)? Think Again*. New York: John Wiley & Sons, Inc., 2009.

Robbins, Anthony. *Unlimited Power: The New Science of Personal Achievement*. New York: Simon & Schuster, 1986.

Schneider, Bruce D. *Energy Leadership: Transforming Your Workplace and Your Life from the Core*. New York: John Wiley & Sons, 2007.

Schneider, Bruce D. *Relax, You're Already Perfect: 10 Spiritual Lessons to Remember*. Charlottesville, VA: Hampton Roads Publishing Co., 2002.

Schneider, Jakob Robert. *Family Constellations: Basic Principles and Procedures*. Heidelberg: Carl Auer International, 2007.

Seligman, Martin E. P., *Authentic Happiness: Using the New Positive Psychology to Realize Your Potential for Lasting Fulfillment*. New York: Free Press, 2004.

Seligman, Martin E. P., *Learned Optimism: How to Change Your Mind and Your Life*. New York: Free Press, 1998.

Stober, Diane R., Grant, Anthony M., *Evidence Based Coaching Handbook: Putting Best Practices to Work for Your Clients*. New York: Free Press, 1998.

Wright, Kurt, *Breaking the Rules: Removing the Obstacles to Effortless High Performance*. CPM Publishing, 1998.